THE DETOX SERIES

Seven Sermons on Decontaminating the Soul

INCLUDES: 31 DAILY INSPIRATIONAL NUGGETS

THE DETOX SERIES

Seven Sermons on Decontaminating the Soul

INCLUDES: 31 DAILY INSPIRATIONAL NUGGETS

Larry A. Brookins

authorHOUSE®

AuthorHouse™
1663 Liberty Drive
Bloomington, IN 47403
www.authorhouse.com
Phone: 1-800-839-8640

Published by AuthorHouse 4/2/2014

ISBN: 978-1-4969-0257-3 (sc)
ISBN: 978-1-4969-0256-6 (e)

Library of Congress Control Number: 2014906265

Cover imagery: CanStockPhoto 1972307, www.CanStockPhoto.com

I dedicate this book to all who are endeavoring to live an authentic life and to you who are suffering from low self-esteem, who feel the need to be validated and accepted by others, who live your life by the script that others have written for you. May you find in these pages sufficient inspiration and strength to be set free to be who God created you to be—your genuine self. May this book equip you to examine yourself and to excavate from yourself all toxic elements lodged within the storage faculties of your mind, will, and emotions, which comprise your soul— and may it help you to rid from the circle of your associations and environment all harmful relationships and connections that inhibit and hamper you from embracing life in such a way that you enjoy life. My prayer for you is that of the Apostle John: *"Beloved, I wish above all things that thou mayest prosper and be in health, even as thy soul prospereth"* (3 John 1:2). To you, who want to live for God, this book is earmarked. Be blessed!

CONTENTS

INTRODUCTION

How did we get here? This book is the progeny of a God-inspired movement that began when I challenged the congregation where I serve as Senior Pastor, *True Foundation Transformation Church* (Chicago), to journey with me on a 40 day look at ourselves, with the goal of ridding from our lives all things toxic, both within us and around us—the things and people that inhibit and divert us from being all that God created us to be, and the things and people found to be an obstruction to our quest of becoming our authentic or genuine self.

On January 19th, 2014, we began a 40-day self and soul treatment of internal and external examination and excavation by reading the book, *The 40 Day Soul Fast* (Cindy Trimm). This book served as the catalyst of our transformational endeavor. I highly recommend it. This was a fast, not of abstaining from food and beverage, but one geared toward the cleansing of our mind, will and emotions *of* and *from* the various impurities and iniquities we know, or come to know, to be detrimental to our relationship and fellowship with God, as well as to our relationship and camaraderie with others. In fact, we even analyzed and scrutinized the relationships we have with others because we know that some can be the cause of incapacitating one's ability to live life at maximum potential and to embrace life in such a way that we enjoy life. It is true what the Bible says, *"Bad company corrupts good character"* (1 Corinthians 15:33, NIV).

Running with the wrong crowd has desecrated many reputations, perverted too many lives, and has shifted too many destinies from the path of righteousness to that of ungodliness. This is the message of our sermon, *Fatal Attractions*—to avoid, *where* and *when* possible, consorting with individuals of loose morals and principles, delinquent behavior and inclinations, and or with persons that have no reverence of God or relationship with God, other than for the purpose of witnessing to them of the Gospel of Jesus Christ and being before them the 'light of the world' and the 'salt of the earth' that we are called to be as Christians. Never negate the fact that Scripture warns us: *"Be not unequally yoked with unbelievers"* (2

Corinthians 6:14). It also says, *"Come out from among them, and be ye separate, says the Lord"* (2 Corinthians 6:17).

I am so excited over this opportunity to put into publication print the manuscripts of these seven sermons that I know will continue to impact lives for the better as they did when I preached them over the course of seven weeks. I know that the testimonies will too continue of liberation and edification, and I pray, illumination and motivation. Motivation to make a visit to the Potter's house and to take a sit on the Potter's wheel and allow the Hands of God to mold and shape or remold and reshape your thoughts, will, emotions, character, conduct, communication, and conversations, as well as your desire to live for Him in this world and before this world. Motivation to say to God: 'Lord, clean this house from the inside out', and to say to Him, as David did: *"Create in me a clean heart, O God, and renew a right spirit within me"* (Psalm 51:10).

There is no greater joy in the eyes of God then to see a life that is consecrated unto Him. Know that; as your life is pleasing to God, it becomes rewarding for you. It is written, *"No good thing will He withhold from them that walk uprightly"* (Psalm 84:11). *"Take delight in the LORD, and He will give you the desires of your heart"* (Psalm 37:4). I believe that there is always divine compensation for human consecration. Proverbs 16:7 says, *"When people's lives please the LORD, even their enemies are at peace with them"* (NLT). It does pay to live for God, both in this temporal realm of our existence, as well as in the Eternal Home God has prepared for those who love Him, once we leave here.

I've included in this book 31 daily inspirational nuggets that too were given life through our 40-day pilgrimage to personal purification. During the course of the 40 days that we were reading the book, *The 40 Day Soul Fast* (Cindy Trimm), I posted these wisdom words on my Facebook page and received many thankful commentaries for having done so. As with the sermon manuscripts, I pray that these daily thoughts can encourage you, and awaken you, and enlighten you, and perhaps, if need be, convict you of any *sin* or *sins* against God, yourself, and others. I pray that the labor we poured into writing them will be poured into you and produce within you an even greater appreciation for life, as well as an enhanced love and admiration for the blessings and grace bestowed upon each of us, each and every day by God. It is my prayer your daily walk will be a little more invigorated because of these nuggets of inspiration.

One final thing; I wrote what I call, a *Prayer and Pledge of Participation*, distributed a copy to all who involved themselves with us on our 40-day spiritual expedition and exploration, and I asked them to read it every day to themselves prior to reading the assigned chapter for the day. It too, I have placed in this book following this introductory section, that you too may experience, to some degree, what 'they' and 'I' experienced during the period of January 19th through February 27th, 2014.

I thank you for purchasing this book, but even more, I thank God for granting me the privilege of being used by Him as a vessel of His will. In all I do and become it is, at all times, because of Him, and for that I will always be grateful. Thus we say, *to God Be the Glory for what He has done and continues to do.*

Living in the Overflow of Calvary,
Rev. Dr. Larry A. Brookins

PRAYER AND PLEDGE
OF PARTICIPATION

May this fast be a time of purification for me, as
I seek truth and clarity about myself and God's
purpose for my life. May this fast be a time of
Divine encounter, allowing me to experience the
presence and power of God in my life and through
my life. May it awaken me to all things within me
in need of purging from me, and may it arouse
me to pour into me what I need to be a better me.
I do this fast for inner cleansing. I do this fast to
bring out of me my authentic self: to decontaminate
my thoughts, will, emotions, character, actions,
words, and values, and to feast on the spiritual
truths of God's Word, as I seek to apply them to
my life and limbs. This is my desire, and this is
my quest for the next 40 days. I know that when
all is well with my soul, then all will be well with
my surroundings, no matter the situations.

CHAPTER ONE – SERMON ONE

OPERATION DETOX

REV. DR. LARRY A. BROOKINS
(First Preached - True Foundation Transformation Church - 1/19/14)

Mark 7:14-23 & Ephesians 4:29; 31-32
(New King James Version)

MARK 7:14-23

[14] When He had called all the multitude to *Himself,* He said to them, "Hear Me, everyone, and understand: [15] There is nothing that enters a man from outside which can defile him; but the things which come out of him, those are the things that defile a man. [16] If anyone has ears to hear, let him hear!" [17] When He had entered a house away from the crowd, His disciples asked Him concerning the parable. [18] So He said to them, "Are you thus without understanding also? Do you not perceive that whatever enters a man from outside cannot defile him, [19] because it does not enter his heart but his stomach, and is eliminated, *thus* purifying all foods?" [20] And He said, "What comes out of a man, that defiles a man. [21] For from within, out of the heart of men, proceed evil thoughts, adulteries, fornications, murders, [22] thefts, covetousness, wickedness, deceit, lewdness, an evil eye, blasphemy, pride, foolishness. [23] All these evil things come from within and defile a man."

EPHESIANS 4:29; 31-32

29 Let no corrupt word proceed out of your mouth, but what is good for necessary edification, that it may impart grace to the hearers.

31 Let all bitterness, wrath, anger, clamor, and evil speaking be put away from you, with all malice.

32 And be kind to one another, tenderhearted, forgiving
one another, even as God in Christ forgave you.

Today, we begin our journey to authentic living as we glean from the book, THE 40 DAY SOUL FAST, written by Cindy Trimm. The object of this 40-day fast is not so much the abstinence of food and beverage, but the cleansing of the various impurities within us that are detrimental to our thoughts, and desires, and character, and affections, and those things that are hindrances to us living our best life possible.

Per the author, this 40-day soul fast "is a transformational expedition that will lead you [I insert 'us'] on an inward journey to greater health, happiness, and success as you [I insert 'we'] learn to live from the inside out." Per the author, the goal is "to guide you/us through the process of discovering who you/we really are," helping us to identify things within us in need of purging from us and helping us to clear away all detected pollutants that incapacitate our abilities to operate within life at maximum capacity or to embrace life in such a way that we enjoy life.

A lot of people cannot embrace life and do not enjoy life simply because of the unrest on the inside, and what affects us on the inside will affect us on the outside. In other words, if there is no peace within, there will be no peace without. In the book it is written: "When you have peace in your soul, you will bring that peace to bear on the world around you."

Through our invitation to you to join us for the next 40 days, we are seeking to help you to eliminate those things within you that cripple you from feeling good about yourself, and from being all that God designed you to be, and from doing all that you are capable of doing, if you are healthy on the inside. Sickness, in any form, has a tendency of slowing us down, altering our emotions, inhibiting our activities, and delaying our destinies. A question is asked on page 27: "Could things be the way they are because you are the way you are?" Many of us have heard the phrase, *"Misery loves company,"* and what that phrase mean is that, "people, who are unhappy, like other people to be unhappy too." In other words, if you are sad, you want other people to be sad. In other words, if things are not quite right with you, in your life, in your relationship, with your finances, et cetera, then such people tends to wish the same on others, and some do what they can to even inflict the same on others. Yes, misery loves company.

The 40 Day Soul Fast is about learning how to live free from negativity, and free from self-doubt, and free from fear, and free from shame, and free from self-condemnation, and free from façade or pretense, and free from living by the expectations of others, or other self-imposed barriers that constrain our growth and enslave our soul. The 40 Day Soul Fast will help us to look within ourselves with the intent of changing the trajectory of our life by changing what we allow to remain in us and what we sanction to flow out of us. Our text of Ephesians state: *"Let no corrupt word proceed out of your mouth, but what is good for necessary edification." Edification* means: improvement, education, enlightenment, elevation, instruction, and advancement. It is that which builds up and not tears down. It is that which encourages and not discourage. The text goes on to say: *"Let all bitterness, wrath, anger, clamor, and evil speaking be put away from you, with all malice. And be kind to one another, tenderhearted, forgiving one another, even as God in Christ forgave you."* Here's a lesson: Some things around us are beyond our control, but what's in us, that comes out of us, or remains in us, we can change. The *Serenity Prayer* of Reinhold Niebuhr (KNEE-bore) says: "God, grant me the serenity to accept the things I cannot change, the courage to change the things I can, and the wisdom to know the difference." The Bible says, *"If any of you lacks wisdom, you should ask God, who gives generously to all without finding fault, and it will be given to you"* (James 1:5). Filter out the bad and take in what is good.

Oftentimes we give much attention to the outward us, but not enough deliberation or concentration to the inward us, and it's the inward us that needs more therapy than the outward us. In our text of Mark Jesus says, and I'm paraphrasing: *"It is not what goes into us that defiles us, but what comes out of us that causes contamination, not only within us, but also around us."* Cindy Trimm says: "It's not about what you're eating, but what's eating you." My interpretation is: in a physical fast it is about what you ingest, but in a soul fast it is about what you regurgitate. "What's eating you?" In other words, what is it on the inside that needs elimination? I told the church on Thursday night that a bowel movement is critical in ejecting from us what could be harmful to us, if permitted to remain, and so it is in the natural, so it is in the spiritual, as well as with our emotions. Many of us are stressed out, and stress invades our life through the pressures of life that we allow to penetrate into our soul and constipate us, and all we need for relief is release.

An unhealthy surrounding is many times the spin-off of an unhealthy soul, soul consisting of 'mind,' 'will,' and 'emotion,' and like a dirty house needs housecleaning, every now and then the inner us need disinfection to liquidate out of us all that is hazardous to us, and all that prohibits us from embracing and enjoying the peace that God wants us to have.

The clinical term is *detoxification*, which is defined as *"the process of removing toxic substances or qualities,"* whether in us or around us. Where found, that which is toxic must be detoxified, or else, it can infect and affect us in an unfavorable way.

In the foreword to the book, *The 40 Day Soul Fast*, Bishop TD Jakes states: "All of us need to detox our inner man from negativity, carnality, and [from] the memories of past hurts and pain, which act like a virus in our mind and a cancer within our soul." In other words, instead of spending time dissecting what's wrong with everybody else, we need to spend time with ourselves and on ourselves; as Michael would say: 'It starts with the man in the mirror.' Before we can produce change around us, there must be a metamorphosis within us. *Fasting* is personal. The journey to a different you must originate with you and you must focus on you. The Bible says, *"Let a man examine himself."* In other words, stop looking at me and start looking at yourself. The Williams' Brothers would say: "Sweep around your own front door before you try to sweep around mine."

We're only 19 days into this New Year and now is the right time to work on a new you. Now is the right time for all of us to do some in-house inventory—for all of us to take stock of the good and of the bad, and to discard the bad and enhance the good. *Discard* means *"to get rid of,"* or *"to reject as no longer useful or desirable,"* and before you go home and pack up your spouse's stuff, let me clarify.

Indeed, there are some people in our lives that should no longer be in our lives, and indeed, there are some relationships that are toxic and in need of severance, but even if you get rid of them and don't work on yourself, the ailments on the inside will eventually

4

resurface. Yes, sometimes, it's the people around us, but many times, it's the person within us, and unless you purify you, someone new in your life is not the answer. In fact, many new relationships have been damaged by the residue of the old, as we make others responsible for the baggage we brought along. It's the same concept with people who move from church to church to church to church, always finding fault in others, when the faultiness is within. Nobody's perfect. You're not perfect, so why are you looking for perfection all around you when it is not in you.

Let me give some advice to anyone contemplating a move to someone new or a move to some place different. Make sure it's not you. Make sure you can live with you before you invite somebody else to live with you. Don't bring somebody else into your world of chaos, crazy, and confusion. Make sure you're healthy before you connect someone else to you, inclusive of children.

Can I be honest? Some people are not ready to have children. They are unstable, immature, unemployed, and narcissistic, and too many children suffer because of the discombobulation, dysfunction, and conceitedness of the parent and/or parents.

Can I give some advice? Get yourself together first. Get your finances together first. Get your emotions together first. Get your life in order first. Grow up yourself before you attempt to raise another human. I'm not judging anybody. We all make mistakes, but let's not bring kids into our realm of unreadiness and unhealthiness.. We only make matters worse.

Whether you think so or not, all of us have issues, and all of us have defects, and all of us have idiosyncrasies, and some trash within us that is in need of disposal, and whether you think so or not, all of us, from time-to-time, are in need of detoxification. If there's bitterness on the inside, you need detoxification. If there's anger on the inside, you need detoxification. If it's unforgiveness, you need detoxification. If it's hatred, you need detoxification. You need a spiritual enema to purge these toxins out of you.

Resentment is toxic. Jealousy is toxic. Envy is toxic, and malice is toxic. They are venomous sentiments that can destroy you from the inside out, if they remain in you. It's time for OPERATION DETOX. Can't let go of the past, it's time. Can't live in the present, it's time. You're mad at the world, it's time. Don't have one friend, it's time. It's time to free yourself from constipation. It's time to free yourself from agitation. "Free yourself, so you can be yourself." Cleanse yourself on the inside, so you can live your life on the outside.

Come journey with us. Let's get healthy. Come journey with us. Let's get whole. Come journey with us. Let's get delivered. Come journey with us. Let's get healed. "It's time."

It's time for transformation. It's time for purification. It's time for decontamination. It's time for OPERATION DETOX. "For the next 40 days I'm in treatment. For the next 40 days I'm in therapy. For the next 40 days I'm in counseling. For the next 40 days I am analyzing me from the inside out." I'm on a soul fast and I'm cleaning house. I'm on a soul fast and it's coming out. It's coming out so I can be what God created me to be. It's coming out so I can live life on God's terms. So I can smile again. So I can laugh again. So I can love again. So I can put the past in the past, and live in the present, and reach for my future. It's coming out so I can say to myself, "It is well with my soul." No matter the condition around me, "It is well with my soul!"

CHAPTER TWO – SERMON TWO

THINKING POSITIVE THOUGHTS

REV. DR. LARRY A. BROOKINS
(First Preached – True Foundation Transformation Church – 1/26/14)

Philippians 4:8
(King James Version)

Finally, brethren, whatsoever things are true,
whatsoever things are honest, whatsoever
things are just, whatsoever things are pure,
whatsoever things are lovely, whatsoever things
are of good report; if there be any virtue, and if
there be any praise, think on these things.

Today is Day 8 of our 40-day soul fast and as we continue our quest to becoming our authentic self, or as we continue our journey to becoming true to who we really are in alignment with who God created us to be and what the Word of God says about us, in that, we are *"fearfully and wonderfully made"* (Psalm 139:14), I want to turn our attention to, perhaps, the most critical dimension of the soul, which is our mind. Of course, the *soul* is comprised of mind, will and emotions, but it is from the mind where the directives for what we do and how we feel are dispatched. The mind gives leadership to every part of the body; organs, tissues, and cells await a signal or message from the mind. The mind is the hub of movement and affection and it is the epicenter of deliberation or thought. *Thought* determines mood and thought dictates agenda. It, or they, manipulates words, shapes character, formulates personality, constructs temperament, and facilitates one's progress in life and through life.

So we know how critical our thoughts are; if our thoughts cease to function, so do we. In fact, when such happens in the physical, clinically, we are labeled "brain dead," which is a term that addresses the irreversible end of brain activity that is necessary for body function and necessary to sustain life. Many doctors would tell you, if there is no activity in the brain, for the most part, 'life support,' in essence, becomes 'death support.'

On page 74 of Cindy Trimm's book, *The 40 Day Soul Fast*, there is a quote from the Roman Emperor, *Marcus Aurelius Antoninus*, which states: "Our life is what our thoughts make it." In other words, your thoughts order your reality. In other words, everything that occurs in your life is interpreted by the thoughts of your mind. In other words, by your thoughts you add meaning to your life, and, by your thoughts you add the emotional response to what occurs in your life. In fact, by your thoughts you regulate the temperature of your disposition and, by your thoughts, you decide what reaction you have to what happens in your day, week, month, or year, be what happens good or bad, joyous or tragic.

I told you last week that 'you' are in control of 'you', and with this in mind; know that—your thoughts are the steering wheel that navigates the direction you take in life. They are the part of us that affects everything else about us, and in this, you cannot allow anyone else to take control of your wheel; you must hold it yourself and drive yourself.

When you can drive yourself and when you have your own car, you don't have to depend on anyone else and wait around for anyone else to take you where you need to go—you can grab your own keys and drive your own self. Depending on others puts them in control of you, and it inhibits you, and sometimes, it inhibits them. They can't do what they need to do or want to do because they have to drive you—I say: get your own. Get your own car. Get your own house. Get your own money. Get your own life. I make this latter statement, "Get your own life," because; with some people, their whole life is wrapped up in somebody else's life, and what happens when there is a separation, or divorce, or the inevitable—death? They can't cope. They can't function. They can't handle affairs. They cannot manage their own lives. I say again: get your own. Learn how to cook for yourself. Learn how to dress yourself. Learn how to think for yourself. Learn how to be yourself. Stop depending on everybody around you to get you where you need to go, and stop depending on everybody around you to make decisions for you. It's your life. Think for yourself. Make up your own mind. You know, in this day of lawsuit frenzy, you've got to be careful giving advice to others because, if things don't work out for them and they did what you told them to do, they will turn around and sue you for the advice you gave them. Make up your own mind.

As we continue the inner detox process, the lesson we must learn today is the importance of what we think, not what others think, but what we think. I know the Bible teaches us that *"in the multitude of counsel there is safety,"* and it is, but too often, we depend too much on what other people think. Proverbs 23:7 declares, *"For as he thinks in his heart, so is he."* The late British philosophical writer *James Allen* interprets it this way: "They themselves are makers of themselves by virtue of the thoughts which they choose and encourage."

Our thoughts make us what we are. If we think failure, we will fail. If we think lack, we will lack. If we think depression, we will be depressed. If we focus on the negative, we will be negative. Negative actions and reactions are the offspring of negative thoughts. A worried mind leads to a worried life, and a worried life can lead to nervous breakdown and suicidal tendencies. Think positive thoughts. If we think happy, we will be happy. If we think we can, most likely, we will. If we think with confidence, we will act in confidence, and if we focus on what we do have, we will recognize just how blessed we really are.

I want to say to somebody: 'Stop looking at the glass half empty; is it not half full?' The text says: *"Whatsoever things are true, whatsoever things are honest, whatsoever things are just, whatsoever things are pure, whatsoever things are lovely, whatsoever things are of good report; if there be any virtue* [or advantage], *and if there be any praise* [or something that is commendable], *think on these things."* In other words, let your thoughts steer you to the up side and not the down side. Let them have you concentrating on and contemplating the better things in your life instead of the worse things of your life. All of us have problems. All of us have bills. All of us have questions, and all of us will die, but to His faithful followers Jesus says, *"In Me, you can have peace,"* and our faith reassures us that after death comes life. Think on that.

Think on the positive. Think on the progressive. Think on

the triumphs. Think on your testimonies, and if the Lord did it before, somebody's got to think that He will do it again. Oftentimes we forget, or we put out of our minds, the hurdles we've already overcome and the God who made it possible. *Tye Tribett* would say, "If He did it before, He can do it again; same God right now, same God back then."

The problem with many of us is that we give too much attention to the flaws of life, when all of life has flaws. Nothing and nobody is perfect. If you're looking for imperfection you will find it, for imperfection is all around us, as well as in us. Have you looked in the mirror lately? We all have them. I said last week: "You're not perfect, so why are you demanding perfection in everybody around you, when perfection is not in you." Let's get out the broom again: "Sweep around your own front door before you try to sweep around mine." I must say again: "Stop looking at the glass half empty." Think about what you have and thank God for what you have. Want more or something different? If you change the way you think, you will change your life. Want more or something different? Your thoughts can transform your world.

Stop feeling sorry for yourself and start thinking better thoughts about yourself, and stop allowing the opinions of others about you to deteriorate or depreciate what you think about you. Raise your own self-esteem. What you think about yourself is far more important than what other people think about you. We give too much authority to the viewpoints of others about us, and not enough to what we think about ourselves. I heard Bishop Noel Jones say: *"Don't allow people to limit you by their negative opinions of you."* He said, *"Shut them up, and if you can't shut them up, shut them out."* In other words, condition your environment.

Cindy Trimm says in her book, *"A fast is about exchanging something of lesser value for something of greater value,"* and I say, what you think about you is more valuable than the surveys that others conduct on you. In one sense you do care, but in another, you must not care. Condition your environment. Eliminate from your thoughts the toxins of negativity, pessimism, and low self-esteem, and if it's around you, then remove yourself from 'it' or 'them', or 'them' and 'it' from you. Amputate all carriers of disapproval, condemnation, agitation, and cynicism. Delete every mocker. Disconnect every skeptic. Break away from every belittler, and all life-sapping agents. Enhance your thoughts of you with the right people around you. You need people around you that will encourage you. You need people around you that will support you. You need people around you that will inspire you. You need people in your circle of connection that are healthy for you. The Bible says, *"Evil communication corrupts good manners."* Stop hanging out with the wrong people. If you want to be better, upgrade your surroundings.

You cannot be true to yourself when you are always concerned with the thoughts of others about you. I cannot be me trying to be what you think I should be. Standing in the lyrics of "I've Got to be me," I've got to be me. I appreciate your input, but I want to be what God wants be to be. I want to do what God wants me to do. I want to say what God wants me to say. I want to live how God wants me to live. I've got to be me. You do you and let me do me.

Don't let people distract you from God's purpose for you. Renew your mind. Readjust your thinking. Revamp your thoughts, and modify your associations. There is some good in you. Make sure there is some good around you. Paul says, *"Think on these things."*

Think on what's good about your life. Think on what's right in your life. *If there be any virtue and if there be any praise, think on these things.* Highlight the good. Accentuate the positive. Override every bad thought with a good thought and countermand every negative one with positive ones.

We've got 32 more days to make a turnaround for the better, so get in your cocoon and let the Holy Spirit do His work. Get in there and let Him purify your thoughts. Get in there and let Him clean up your life. Get in there and let Him change you from the inside out. Get in there so that old things can pass away, so that all things can become new. Reclaim your mind. Regenerate your thoughts. Recondition your thinking. Overhaul your connections. *"Let this mind be in you, which was also in Christ Jesus."*

THINK POSITIVE THOUGHTS! It will make a difference in your life. THINK POSITIVE THOUGHTS! They will turn your life around. THINK POSITIVE THOUGHTS! You can make it if you do it. THINK POSITIVE THOUGHTS and everything will be alright!

CHAPTER THREE – SERMON THREE

DO YOU WANT TO BE MADE WHOLE?

REV. DR. LARRY A. BROOKINS
(First Preached – True Foundation Transformation Church – 2/2/14)

John 5:1-9(a)
(King James Version)

After this there was a feast of the Jews; and Jesus went up to Jerusalem. [2] Now there is at Jerusalem by the sheep market **[sheep gate]** a pool, which is called in the Hebrew tongue Bethesda, having five porches. [3] In these lay a great multitude of impotent folk **[sick people]**, of blind, halt **[lame]**, withered **[paralyzed]**, waiting for the moving of the water. [4] For an angel went down at a certain season **[time]** into the pool, and troubled **[stirred up]** the water: whosoever then first stepped in **[whoever stepped in first]** after the troubling **[stirring up]** of the water was made whole of whatsoever disease he had. [5] And a certain man was there, which had an infirmity thirty and eight years **[thirty-eight years]**. [6] When Jesus saw him lie **[lying there]**, and knew that he had been now a long time in that case **[that he already had been in that condition a long time]**, He saith **[said]** unto him, Wilt thou be made whole **[do you want to be made whole]**? [7] The impotent **[sick]** man answered him, Sir, I have no man, when the water is troubled **[stirred up]**, to put me into the pool: but while I am coming, another steppeth down **[steps down]** before me. [8] Jesus saith **[said]** unto him, Rise; take up thy bed, and walk. [9] And immediately the man was made whole, and took up his bed, and walked:"

Today is Day 15 of our 40-day soul fast and our message has its basis in our reading of Day 7, where the subject is 'healing' and the characteristic is 'wholeness'. *Wholeness*, Day 7 defines as: "Living in such a way that all facets and aspects of our lives are interrelated in a physically fit, nutritionally healthy, emotionally sound, spiritually congruent, socially moral, professionally ethical, mentally resilient, and financially adept way." It states that; "wholeness is the opposite of brokenness."

Brokenness is seen as being in a state of disarray, confusion, disorder, and dysfunction—simply put, that, which is broken, is incomplete. In other words, it is lacking something. In other words, it is deficient of something. In other words, it is in need of something in order to be complete, and in order to be unbroken, and in order to be undamaged—in order to be whole.

Brokenness will prevent you from living your life at its maximum potential. It unbalances your life. It de-energizes your passions. It unhinges your self-esteem, and it creates chaos in your environment. We stated in the flagship sermon of this series, *Operation Detox*, that 'what affects us on the inside will affect us on the outside.'

Hurting people tend to emit hurt and the disappointed will disappoint. "Misery loves company." When you're broken, your brokenness infects your surroundings. It contaminates. It taints, and it impacts, negatively, everything that it comes in contact with. *Brokenness* is contagious. It is detrimental. It is harmful. It is damaging. It is toxic.

We live in a world of brokenness. We live in a world of dis—ease. We live in a world of malfunction. We live in a world of break down and break up.

Brokenness is caused by many things. Sickness leads to breakage. Disappointment leads to breakage. Divorce leads to breakage, and death leads to breakage. Unfulfilled dreams lead to breakage. A shortage of money leads to breakage. Unexpected calamities lead to breakage, and severed friendships and relationships can leave you emotionally broken.

There are many people walking around with various conditions of brokenness—some from pains and hurts within their past and some from agonizing predicaments within their present; and some of them are some of us, who are fixed up on the outside, but broken down on the inside—dressed up externally, but messed up internally—smiling, but sad—singing, but shattered—clapping, but crushed—dancing, but depressed.

We're here, but we're broken. We have on our uniforms, but we're broken. We have wounds that have left us impotent, wounds that have left us immobilized, wounds that have left us traumatized, and wounds that have left us disheartened. We have no joy. We have no peace. We are not happy. We are just here. Like the man lying by the pool of Bethesda—just here, watching others get healed—just here, watching others get whole—just here watching others receive their breakthrough—just here, in the same condition we've been in for a long time; at home and in church living a life of incarceration—at home and in church living a life of stagnation—at home and in church living a life of desolation—at home and in church living a life of fragmentation.

We're *here* or *there*, but detached. We're *here* or *there*, but our hearts are fractured, and our spirits are low, and our will is handicap, and our emotions are on the brink of a nervous breakdown. The question is asked, "Do you want to be made whole?" In other words, do you want to come out of the rut you find yourself in? Are you tired of living life in a holding pattern? Are you weary of feeling empty, unfulfilled, frustrated and dissatisfied? The question of *do you want to be made whole* is a good question because; *wholeness* cannot come unless you want it. It is difficult to help somebody when that person doesn't want to be helped. In many cases, it is only when they decide for themselves that they need help and want help that they can truly be helped.

Many of us have heard it said, "You can lead a horse to water, but you can't make it drink." In other words, you can present opportunity, but *unless* and *until* the opportunity is embraced, the advantage of opportunity is wasted. People, like horses, will only do what they have a mind to do or truly want to do. I can introduce opportunity to you, but I cannot force it on you. I can give advice to you, but I cannot force it on you. I can share the Will and Word of God with you, but I cannot force it on you. This is why I say, from time-to-time, my job is to simply put it out there; it's up to you to grab hold of it and to do something with it. Transformation comes through application.

If you really want change in your life there is a Change-Agent for your life, but He will not invade your life—you must invite Him in. Jesus says, *"Behold, I stand at the door and knock, and if any man open up the door I'll come in."* "Do you want to be made whole?" Not everyone who begs for money for something to eat will use that money for something to eat. Do you want to be made whole? *Wholeness* is beneficial. *Wholeness* is advantageous. *Wholeness* is auspicious. *Wholeness* is for the best. Cindy Trimm says in her book: "When you operate from a place of wholeness, you strengthen your position to field any kind of ball that comes your way." In other words, when you are whole, you can handle whatever life brings to pass in your life. In other words, you can deal with difficulty, you can cope with crisis, you can survive storms, and you will not crumble, fall to pieces, crack up, or lose control.

I've been telling you for the last couple of weeks that; *you are in control of you*, but when you allow other things and or other people to wear down your resistance level; you open yourself up to all forms of viruses that attack the health of your mind, body, emotions, and will.

Viruses are infective agents that seek to corrupt, deteriorate, incapacitate, and steal whatever they can from you. A *virus* will steal your health. A *virus* will steal your happiness. A *virus* will steal your hopefulness, and it will steal your desire to live.

It can be devastating and discouraging going through life without seeing any improvement in your life: day after day, week after week, month after month, year after year—still in the same place, still in the same position, still in the same predicament, still in the same condition—feeling unloved, feeling ineffective, feeling overwhelmed, feeling overlooked, feeling isolated, and feeling as if nobody cares. But I have some good news. *Wholeness* is the fruit of God's grace. If you want to be made whole, you can be made whole. If you want to be healed, you can be healed. If you want to be delivered, you can be delivered. If you wanted to be mended, you can be mended. If you want to be set free, you can be set free.

It does not matter how long you've been coming to the pool. It does not matter if you never get in the pool. It does not matter if no one helps you to the pool. The question is: "Do you want to be made whole?" If so, there is help. If so, there is hope. If so, there is treatment. If so, there is JESUS. He's here to fix you up. He's here to help you out. He's here to remedy your condition. He's here to make you whole.

Whatever you need healing from, give it to Jesus. If it's relational, give it to Jesus. If it's emotional, give it to Jesus. If it's financial, give it to Jesus. If it's physical, give it to Jesus. If you surrender, He can save you. If you believe, He can heal you. If you trust, He can rebuild you; just turn 'you' over to the Lord.

Substance abuse, turn it over. Alcoholism, turn it over. Pornography, turn it over. Promiscuity, turn it over. Let go of every toxin that is inhibiting your wholeness.

Unforgiveness—let it go! Resentment—let it go! Bitterness—let it go! Anger—let it go! Make a visit to the Potter's house and take a seat on the Potter's wheel. God can make you whole. God can repair your life. God can purify your defects. God can decontaminate your soul. He is the Potter, we are the clay, let Him mold you and reshape you, let the LORD have His way. Do you want to be better? Do you want to live holy? Do you want to please Him? DO YOU WANT TO BE MADE WHOLE?

CHAPTER FOUR – SERMON FOUR

WE ARE WHAT WE THINK

REV. DR. LARRY A. BROOKINS
(First Preached – True Foundation Transformation Church – 2/9/14)

Proverbs 23:7(a)
(New King James Version)

"For as he thinks in his heart, so is he"

Today is Day 22 of our 40-day soul fast and I want to revisit a theme that was the focal point of our sermon two Sundays ago, which was entitled, *"Thinking Positive Thoughts."* Do you remember that? There, in Part 2 of our current Detox series, we highlighted the importance of our thought life as we sought to communicate to you the necessity of readjusting and redirecting our thoughts from what is absent within our lives to what is present in our lives, and from giving too much attention and authority to the opinions of others about us, to celebrating and enhancing what we think about ourselves. It's about self-validation.

If you remember I stated: "What we think about ourselves is far more important than the surveys of others done on us." In fact, there are some people who will appraise you, when they don't even know you. I say; give no credence to the evaluations of others—of greater value than theirs are the appraisals we give ourselves. In fact, it is the thoughts we have of ourselves that are the very things that either make us or break us, not the contemplation or conversations of others, but it is the assessment of self-contemplation that becomes the pivotal factor on whether or not we feel good about ourselves. If you don't think good of yourself, you will not feel good about yourself. This is why you cannot relinquish your feelings to someone else.

Our feelings are aspects of our emotions, but our emotions are

17

governed by our thoughts. Others can state their perspectives, but in the final analysis, what truly matters is self-perspective. In the final analysis what truly matters is—what YOU think about YOU?

In the final analysis, we control us. In the final analysis, we define us. In the final analysis, we determine us. In the final analysis, it is the internal voice of the mind and not the external voices of our surroundings that regulate our behavior and disposition.

In the final analysis, we are what we think. In the final analysis, we do what we think. In the final analysis, we say what we think. In the final analysis, we attract what we think. In the final analysis, we become what we think. To paraphrase the late British philosophical writer *James Allen*: 'We ourselves are makers of ourselves by virtue of the thoughts we choose and encourage.' Indeed, we select our thoughts and we incite our thoughts through the things we give permission to come in and reside.

On page 187 of Cindy Trimm's book, *The 40 Day Soul Fast*, it is written: *"The life and reality you are experiencing are a reflection of the thoughts you are thinking,"* and I glean from this that; if we need to change our reality, then we need to change our thoughts. A change of thoughts can change your life, however; oftentimes a change of thought requires a change of the intake of information and imageries that we take in. In other words, we need to guard our thoughts by placing a filter on the perimeters of our mind. In other words, we must better select the material we read, the material we watch, the material we listen to, and the material we ponder.

We deceive ourselves if we think that what we watch on TV, see at the movies, listen to on our IPods, play on our gaming systems, and read before bedtime doesn't affect us. In reality, it does. Each image and message we ingest becomes a 'tenant' or 'squatter' in our minds, therefore; if we are serious about our spiritual house-cleaning and soul fast, then we must also take seriously the images, and the languages, and the stories that we allow into our minds, for just as much as internal thoughts are persuasive to external activities, so outside sources are influential to inside deliberations. The two are mutually instrumental for good or bad.

On one side, a corrupt environment can lead to corrupt considerations, while on the other side, corrupt considerations can lead to corrupt conduct. Viewing X-rated movies creates an X-rated mind, and an X-rated mind wants to do X-rated things. Listening to vulgar music induces vulgarity of thought, which in turn propels obscenity of speech. It starts on the inside but is influenced by the outside. We are what we think; therefore, our thoughts need filtration and detoxification. In other words, we need to purify the meditations of our minds by refining the contents of what we feed our minds.

We enrich our thoughts when we feed our thoughts that which is healthy, moral, decent and righteous, but we debase our thoughts when we serve our thoughts that, which is nasty, wicked, unnatural and inappropriate, and so goes our thoughts, so goes we. The text says, *"For as he thinks in his heart, so is he."* We are what we think. If we enrich our thoughts, we enrich our lives, but if we pervert our thoughts, we pervert our lives. A perverted life is the byproduct of a perverted mind. Right thinking leads to right living. All that we do springs from our thoughts. Whatever we do is first acknowledged by the mind before it is implemented in one's life. To put it another way; what we commit outwardly we embrace inwardly. Action is the procession of thought. Thought is the sculptor that chisels out what our temperament looks like and what our proclivities are bent toward. Be careful of your thoughts. Pray for your thoughts. Be protective of your thoughts, and be aware of what's being formulated in your mind.

In Romans Chapter 1 it talks about a "reprobate mind," and a *reprobate mind* is simply a mind that has become so ingrained in evil and debauchery that its life is not able to stop doing the things that are evil and detestable. It is a mind that has been so inundated with the seeds of sin until it desires no real knowledge of God. It does not seek God's Word. It does not crave God's heart. It does not pursue God's Will. It does not delight in God's Way. It is a mind in rebellion against God that does not concede to or glorify God, and thus a mind that is given *over* and *up* by God to do all forms of unclean things, and a mind that shall receive the compensation for its ways. The Bible says, *"The wages of sin is death,"* and there is no expiration date on this judgment.

Some of us need to be cognizant of the fact that; the more you remove yourself from a study of Scripture, and from fellowship with the saints, and from a regiment of prayer, and from a life in pursuit of holiness—the more your mind becomes reprobate.

The more you walk in the counsel of the ungodly. The more you stand in the way of sinners. The more you sit in the seat of the scornful—the more your mind becomes reprobate.

The more you frequent the whore house, and the liquor store, and the gambling establishment, and associate in practice with drug dealers, gang bangers, pimps and prostitutes—the more your mind becomes reprobate.

People with reprobate minds dishonor their bodies. People with reprobate minds exchange truth for a lie. People with reprobate minds do unnatural things in unnatural ways, and they commit that which is shameful and displeasing to God, justifying such as ethical and irreproachable. *Irreproachable* means, "Beyond criticism" and "without fault". People with reprobate minds turn right wrong and wrong right—in their minds.

"Thought is the index of character." In other words, it catalogues who we really are and it registers our truest intent. Words can be deceptive and a smile can conceal scorn, but your thought reveals the real you. "Man looks on the outward appearance but God looks at the heart." In God's viewpoint, we are not our clothes. We are not what we drive. We are not our jewelry and we are not our bank account. We are what we think.

A dirty man has a dirty mind, even though he has on a clean suit. A loose woman has a loose mind, even though she may wear a fur coat. We are what we think. Our life moves in the direction of thought. Thought steers us and thought pilots us, and if you don't like the direction your life is going, you need to change your thought. In other words, you need a 'renewed mind.' A *renewed mind* is a transformed mind. A *renewed mind* is a rehabilitated mind. A *renewed mind* is a regenerated mind. It is a mind that has been introduced or reintroduced to something other than what it is use to receiving. And if your mind is in need of decontamination and your life of purification, you need the cleanser of God's Word. I hear Paul say, *"I beseech you therefore, brethren, by the mercies of God, that ye present your bodies a living sacrifice, holy, acceptable unto God, which is your reasonable service. And be not conformed to this world: but be ye transformed by the renewing of your mind, that ye may prove what is that good, and acceptable, and perfect, will of God."*

As we've crossed over the halfway mark in our journey of

self-examination and soul sanctification; it's time we weed from our thoughts all things unlike God. It's time we discriminate between right and wrong, between good and evil, between wholesome and unwholesome, between what's clean and what's dirty. It's time.

It's time to disinfect our thoughts. It's time to fumigate our words. It's time to sterilize our steps. It's time to sanitize our lives. We've got 18 more days left to make a turnaround for the better, and my question is: What's on your mind?

The enemy wants your thoughts. If he can have your thoughts, then he has you. We are what we think. We do what we think. We say what we think. We become what we think. What's on your mind? Change the way you think and you change the way you act, for as we think, so we are, and what will help us in our quest for a thought transplant is to set our minds on things above. The Word says, *"Let this mind be in you, which was also in Christ Jesus." "I will keep thee in perfect peace whose mind is stayed on Him."* Aim higher in your thought life. Come on up out of the gutter. We are what we think.

CHAPTER FIVE – SERMON FIVE

FATAL ATTRACTIONS

REV. DR. LARRY A. BROOKINS
(First Preached – True Foundation Transformation Church – 2/16/14)

1 Corinthians 15:33
(King James Version)

Be not deceived: evil communications
corrupt good manners.

(New King James Version)
Do not be deceived: "Evil Company
corrupts good habits."

(New International Version)
Do not be misled: "Bad Company
corrupts good character."

INTRODUCTION
Today is Day 29 of our 40 day soul fast,
and as I promised last week, I want to
talk about *"Fatal Attractions"*.

As we've been seeking to detoxify ourselves of elements that are detrimental to the health of our inner being of mind, will, and emotions, one critical area in need of addressing is that of 'association'. By *association*, I mean those close connections that we have with other people—with other people that we are in relationship with— with other people that we claim friendships with—with other people that we allow to speak into our lives, and with the people that walk among our inner circles of frequency and intimacy.

I'm talking about the people that we hang with, and the people that we gang (G-A-N-G) with, and the people that we fall in *love* or *lust* with, and yes, the people that we sleep with: the booty call connections, and the 'friends with benefits' arrangements, and the live-in and live together but not married cohabitations, and all other alliances that may be unwholesome bonds for us and corruptive influences to us, as well as carriers of infectious diseases and demonic spirits.

You do not that demonic spirits are just as contagious as infectious diseases? They, like an STD, flow from one infested person to another where there is romantic contact and or consensus affiliation. We were told years ago: "If you lie down with dogs, you will get up with fleas"—get up *scratching* and *irritated*, simply because; dogs attract fleas. Bernie Mac would say, "Who you with?"

"If you lie down with dogs, you will get up with fleas" is an ancient proverb interpreted meaning, if you associate with bad people, you most likely will acquire their faults. It speaks to us about running with the wrong crowd and the damage it can cause to our character, and the desecration it brings to our reputation.

Another phrase which addresses this is, "guilty by association". To be *guilty by association* invokes the idea of "the attribution or assignment of guilt, without proof, to individuals simply because; the people they associate with is guilty. Under this assertion, you can possibly go to jail by merely being in the congregation or assemblage of criminals, and some people do, not because they themselves broke the law, but because they aligned themselves with lawbreakers.

There is a caution in our text aimed at warning us against keeping company with individuals of loose morals and loose principles, or with people with reputations of delinquent behavior and delinquent inclinations, or with people that are ungodly and wicked, or with people that have no reverence of God or relationship with God. We're going there today.

There is a reason Scripture says to us, *"Be not unequally yoked with unbelievers."* There is a reason Proverbs 13:20 declares, *"He that walks with wise men shall be wise, but a companion of fools shall be destroyed."* There is a reason we are instructed in the opening Book of the

Psalms, not to walk in the counsel of the ungodly, or to stand in the way of sinners, or to sit in the seat of the scornful. There is a reason why it is written in 2nd Corinthians 6:17, *"Come out from among them and be ye separate, says the LORD."*

There is something to be said about the type of people we delight in walking among and who we invite and welcome to walk among us. There is something to be said about the correlation between the people connections we make and the life paths we take. There is a linkage of influence and impact. There is a linkage of confederation and contamination. Association breeds assimilation. 'Birds of a feather tend to flock together.' Let's talk *Fatal Attractions*.

A *fatal attraction* is defined as "an attraction between an individual and someone or something that is so strong that the individual lacks reason and logic in their thinking when dealing with their attraction." It is an attraction that goes beyond normal attraction.

A *fatal attraction* gets to the point where a person may become morbidly infatuated with their love interest to the point where it can get unhealthy and downright dangerous for either party, or for all persons involved.

A *fatal attraction* is any union that is detrimental, toxic, antagonistic, virulent and violent. The liaison is one that may start in pleasure, but ends up in tragedy. It may begin as fun, but it is fun without the thought of ramifications. You cannot give it up to everybody or do it to everybody and not expect some repercussions.

A *fatal attraction* will always have a negative effect and it will leave you with regrets for having gotten involved in the first place. I'm just looking for an honest witness. Are you in the house? You, who have hooked up with someone you wish you never did. You, who slept with somebody you wish you never did. You, who ran with somebody you wish you never did. You, who gave your heart and virginity to somebody you wish you never did. Let's talk *Fatal Attractions*.

I borrowed the phrase from the 1987 movie entitled *Fatal Attraction*, which is a film that centers around a married man who has a weekend affair with a woman who refuses to allow it to end. Uh-huh--you in the house. He, like most men, was only in it for the momentary thrill, but she, like most women, grew emotionally attached, and his rejection of her as something more permanent triggered a catastrophic obsession within her, which pushed her to first slash her wrists, and then pushed her to blackmail, stalking, damaging his car, invading his home, traumatizing his family, making phone calls and hanging up, (you in the house)—boiling the family rabbit in the kitchen, an altercation in another kitchen with a knife, and to a final physical confrontation that left somebody dead. This, indeed, was a fatal attraction that was ignited by the unrestrained passion of sin.

Sin, as it relates to this topic of *fatal attraction*, is sensual gratification that does not give forethought to the consequences of its actions; its only desire is to please itself and to feed the cravings of a flesh that is undisciplined, depraved, perverted, and ill-behaved. Such propensity leads to fornication, adultery, marital separation or divorce, or the contemplation of suicide or homicide.

Some people are so far gone in their mind until they determine within themselves: If I can't have him, or if I can't have her, then nobody will. If this is you, you done lost your mind! You need help. You need therapy. You need treatment. You need Jesus! You need to be on this 40-day soul fast with us. You need detoxification. You need purification. You need regulation. You need a soul enema, for there is something in you that need to come out of you, or there is someone in you in need of exorcism from you.

I must say today that; nobody or nothing is worth losing your mind over. I must say today that; nobody or nothing is worth having a nervous breakdown for. I must say today that; nobody or nothing is worth considering the taking of your own life, and nobody and nothing is worth going to jail for. It ain't that good!

If you are in a toxic relationship, you need to get out. You need to pack your bags. You need to put on your coat. You need to grab your children, and leave. Indeed, *"Evil communication corrupts good manners."* Indeed, *"Evil Company corrupts good habits."* Indeed, *"Bad Company corrupts good character."* Matthew Henry said, "Those who would keep their innocence must keep good company." You falling in love with a thug is a fatal attraction waiting to happen.

Don't stay there and fall apart. Don't stay there and become a victim of domestic violence or spiritual depletion. Don't lose your joy. Don't compromise your salvation. Don't abandon your faith. Don't settle for something less. Raise your expectations. You deserve better. Raise your expectations. You have a right to better. Raise your expectations. God wants to give you better, but you must lift up your standards.

Don't go crazy because they left; sometimes a breakup is a blessing. You may not think so in the moment, but given time you will realize that God was purging your present to preserve your future. God has something better in store for you. I'd rather be by myself than to be with someone who is no good for me.

Stop looking for love in all the wrong places. Stop searching for affection in all the wrong people. The Bible says, *"They that wait upon the LORD shall renew their strength; they shall mount up with wings as eagles; they shall run, and not be weary; and they shall walk, and not faint."*

You need people in your life that will build you up instead of tear you down. You need people that will encourage you. You need people that will complement you. You need people that will consecrate you, and people who love the Lord. If you love Him, you ought to want somebody who loves Him too, for *how can two walk together* if they're walking down different roads, if they're calling on different gods, if they're living by different rules, and if they're hearing a different voice? The Bible says, *"What fellowship has light with darkness"* and *"what part a believer with an unbeliever?"*

We bring trouble on ourselves when we hookup with the wrong crowd, when we hookup with the wrong circle, when we hookup with the wrong clique, when we hookup with the wrong people.

We have eleven days left of detoxification, and it's time to cut some cords. It's time to de-friend some people. It's time to delete some numbers. It's time to deprogram some emotions. Surround yourself with positive vibes and surround yourself with positive people. Make a list and check it twice, and then erase all elements that are hurtful to your life, and detrimental to your godliness, and a hindrance to your potential, and a roadblock to your future.

You don't need a 'Dan' or 'Alex', but someone helpful for your life—someone wholesome for your life—someone constructive for your life—someone favorable for your life. If they're bad news, expunge—if it's stressful, cross it out. Jesus says, *"I am come that they might have life, and that [they might have it] more abundantly."* It's time to live! It's time to clean house! It's time to throw out the garbage. It's time to fumigate and exterminate. It's time to rid ourselves of all things toxic: Toxic relationships, toxic friendships, toxic partnerships, and toxic influences.

I say to you, watch your company and monitor your soul ties. *"Evil communication corrupts good manners." "Evil Company corrupts good habits." "Bad company corrupts good character."* Just because it feels good to you, does not mean that it is good for you. Make that change, so you can feel real good about yourself!

CHAPTER SIX – SERMON SIX

DETOXIFYING THE TONGUE

REV. DR. LARRY A. BROOKINS
(First Preached – True Foundation Transformation Church – 2/23/14)

Ephesians 4:29
(King James Version)
Let no corrupt communication proceed out of your
mouth, but that which is good to the use of edifying,
that it may minister grace unto the hearers.

(New Living Translation)
Don't use foul or abusive language. Let everything
you say be good and helpful, so that your words will
be an encouragement to those who hear them.

As I stated on last week my subject today is
"Detoxifying the Tongue." Detoxify means, "to rid
of poison or the effect of poison." It is the removal
of something that is toxic or something that is
harmful. Our focus today is not on the physical
tongue, but rather on the transmissions of the tongue,
in terms of our language, in terms of our words,
in terms of our talk, in terms of our speech.

Many of us have heard the saying, "Sticks and stones may break
my bones, but words will never hurt me," but to the contrary, words
do hurt. In fact, in many instances the wounds of words can cause
more damage than the wounds inflicted by sticks and stones. In
fact, sometimes the body heals quicker from physical assault than

the mind, will, and emotions do from verbal attack. The redness from a slap will eventually dissipate, but the injuries of harsh words oftentimes permeate. *Permeate* means, "to penetrate through or pass into every part of something." Words penetrate. Words marinate. They flow into our ears and through our ears into our innermost being with some taking up residence in our soul for an extended period of time, immersing with our thoughts and stewing in our hearts. Thus, a word spoken in ten seconds can still have affect after ten years. Think about that for a moment. Think about the long-term impact of what you say.

In James Chapter 3 the tongue is described as "an unruly evil," a small thing that is "full of deadly poison," "a fire," and "a world of iniquity." It is seen as a weapon above all other weapons that has done more damage, split more homes, divided more churches, incapacitated more children, annihilated more reputations, destroyed more relationships, severed more friendships, shattered more livelihoods, and cost more human lives than anything else. The tongue is not made of steel or iron, yet, per Proverbs 12:18, it can pierce like a sword.

Scripture uses the tongue reference to symbolize the communication of our mouths, and such communication is universal. In other words, it is a possession of everyone, regardless of age, wealth, gender, color, or dialect. We are all proprietors of this potentially lethal moving organ that is located in the floor of the mouth. The lips are the door of the mouth but the tongue is what enables us to eat, taste, and speak. Cut out the tongue and you disable one's ability to communicate in an understandable audible way.

As we've arrived at Day 36 of our 40-Day Soul Fast, we turn the spotlight onto the words that come from our mouths through the door of our lips. I know the mind is the hub of all we do and say, and words are indicative of what's in our heart, still, words can be halted or altered at the door of our lips. In other words, we don't have to say what we think and we don't have to say what we feel, we can bridle our tongues, or modify the language of our thoughts, or keep the door of our lips closed.

Many of us were taught, 'If you don't have anything good to say, then don't say anything at all'. In other words, keep your mouth shut. Joel Osteen says, "If you cannot be positive, than at least be quiet."

Mark Twain said, "It is better to keep your mouth closed and let people think you are a fool than to open it and remove all doubt." I say, keep them guessing; don't say a word.

It is written in James 1:19, "Be slow to speak and quick to hear," or *"Quick to hear and slow to speak."* Either way the message is the same: Talk less and listen more. In fact, if we talk less and listen more, we can, perhaps, prevent a lot of arguments, salvage some relationships, maintain some friendships, and stifle some ill-feelings. That's the wise thing to do. Proverbs 17:28 declare, *"Even a fool, when he holds his peace is counted wise: and he that shuts his lips is esteemed a man of understanding."* Sometimes 'silence' is the better option.

Words have life-giving and life-sapping capabilities. Proverbs 18:21 states it this way, *"Death and life are in the power of the tongue."* In other words, your words have authority to unite or separate—to assassinate or amalgamate—to create or destroy—to animate or to decimate.

There is such a thing as wholesome speech and there is such a thing as harmful speech. With our words we can either build up or tear down, we can either hurt or heal, we can either cheer or sadden, and we can either bless or curse. With our words we can mend or rip apart, we can encourage or discourage, we can stabilize or weaken, we can congratulate or infuriate. What comes out is up to us. No one else has control over your lips but you. Thus, before we say a word, we must be cautious and conscientious of every commentary we make and every response we give. In other words, we must think before we talk or contemplate before we converse.

My dad taught us: 'Be careful of what you say because'; it's easy to throw it out there, but difficult to retrieve. I didn't understand it then, but I do now. This advice speaks to the fact that; once you've spoken it, it's not so easy to undo what your words have precipitated or provoked, even *if* or *when* you say, *I'm sorry.* In many instances, the damage is already done, and some damages are irreversible, even if they are forgivable. Once communication is ingrained in the memory bank, it is tough to erase it.

Words are like wounds. Wounds can heal, but with some wounds, a scar remains. I say again, 'sometimes 'silence' is the better option. Ecclesiastes 3:7 declares, *"There is a time to be silent and a time to speak,"* and sometimes when we should speak, we don't speak, and when we shouldn't speak, we do. This is why we need to turn our lips over to the Lord. We pray about everything else, why not ask God, as David does in Psalm 141:3 to *"set a guard over my mouth and put a watch over my lips."* In other words, his prayer, that should be our daily prayer, is to ask the Lord to take control of what we say before we say what we say.

David, like many of us, had an impetuous tempter and sometimes, like many of us, he spoke to quickly without thought and without concern of what his words would stir up, and perhaps, blow up. You do know that we can make matters worse than what they really are when we instigate and agitate with our words. You know, when we nag, and when we badger, and when we persistently, and unrelentingly go on, and on, and on, and on, and on, and on, and on, and on—never letting anything go and never letting anything die; we've got to have the last word; we've got to recap the whole situation; we've got to verbalize every thought; we've got to get out everything that we rehearsed we would say when they got home. But sometimes we need to let it go. Sometimes we need to let God handle it. He can do a better job than we can. In fact, is it not written in Exodus 14:14, *"The LORD will fight for you; you need only to hold your peace?"* But God is not obligated to intervene when we are not willing to muffle our mouth. When you muffle something, you wrap it up. When you muffle something, you put something over it. When you muffle something, you cover it in order to deaden it, repress it, or prevent something from going in or something from coming out of it. In this case, it is to stop us from talking so much—to muffle our sound. Either we muffle it, or where we cannot muffle, we need to put a muzzle on it. We need to do whatever is necessary to zip it up. One commentary states: "the greatest sign of integrity for Christians is not in what we say, but more often in what we do not say."

As Christians we are taught to be Christlike, and a very essential aspect of Christlike character is Christlike conversation. Colossians 4:6 says, *"Let your conversation be gracious and attractive so that you will have the right response for everyone"* (NLT). Christlike conversation probes the question, 'what would Jesus say?' 'How would Jesus answer?' 'What would Jesus' tone be' and 'Would Jesus say anything at all?'

Can you image Jesus saying some of the things that we say? Can you hear Him use the 'B' word? Can you hear Him use the 'N' word? Can you hear Him use the 'S' word? Can you hear Him use the 'F' word, or the 'M.F.' word, or any other form of obscenity, profanity, vulgarity, or crude and rude language? Do you think He would gossip? Do you think He would slander? Do you think He would denigrate? Do you think that Jesus would bear false witness against His neighbor? How about lying? How about backbiting? How about tale-bearing? How about revealing someone else's secrets? How about sarcasm? How about unconstructive criticism? How about exaggeration? What about intimidation? What about foul language? What about abusive language? What about offensive language? How about debilitating language? These are all sins of the tongue that should never flow through the lips of a saint. Years ago, if we said something dirty, mama would say, "Come here; let me wash your mouth out with soap." You want to talk dirty; I've got something for your dirty mouth. Stick out your tongue. Some of us remember those days and some of us need some soap today—with the way we talk, and the way we cuss, and the way we fuss—we need some soap.

As Christians, we have a duty to use our words for edification, and for encouragement, and for education, and for compliments, consolation, salutation and jubilation. We have a duty to build up, and to bless, and to motivate, and inspire; to speak love, to speak peace, to speak hope and support. The text says, *"Let everything you say be good and helpful."* Let it minister grace to the hearer—minister mercy to the hearer—minister kindness to the hearer—minister forgiveness to the hearer—minister joy to the hearer.

Worthless speech doesn't help. Disgusting speech doesn't help. Profane speech doesn't help, and cussing and fussing doesn't help. For the last 35 days, we've been working on our thoughts. Including today, we have 5 days left in our detox program. For the last 35 days, the focus has been on relationships and on environments, and now it's time to work on our words—now it's time to rid ourselves of filthy talk—to rid ourselves of lewd language—to rid ourselves of smutty speech—to rid ourselves of explicit expressions. The Bible says, *"Out of the same mouth proceeds blessing and cursing; these things ought not to be [so]"* (James 3:10); speaking well of someone and speaking badly of someone—praising God and plaguing men—*these things ought not to be so.*

We have the power to use words to speak life into someone's life. I say, therefore; speak life: encourage someone, inspire someone, instruct someone, and edify someone. Don't use words that offend. Don't use words that belittle. Don't use words that inflame. Don't use words that corrupt. It's time to detoxify our tongues—to purify our words—to depollute our language—to decontaminate our talk. We represent the Kingdom of God and must be careful of what we say, how we say it, when we say it, and why we say what we say.

Let my prayer be your prayer; tell the LORD: *"Let the words of my mouth, and the meditation of my heart, be acceptable in Thy sight, O LORD, my Strength, and my Redeemer"* (Psalm 19:14). Let my words edify. Let my words encourage. Let my words provide strength. Let my words speak life!

People are hurting. People are wounded. People are sad—just a word can make a difference in somebody's life. Say that word and make a difference. Say that word and bring healing. Say that word and cheer. Say that word that will put a smile on somebody's face. *"Let no corrupt communication proceed out of your mouth, but that which is good to the use of edifying, that it may minister grace unto the hearers."*

CHAPTER SEVEN – SERMON SEVEN

LORD, CLEAN THIS HOUSE FROM THE INSIDE OUT

REV. DR. LARRY A. BROOKINS
(First Preached – True Foundation Transformation Church – 3/2/14)

Psalm 51:1-10
(King James Version)

Have mercy upon <u>me</u>, O God, according to Thy lovingkindness: according unto the multitude of Thy tender mercies blot out <u>my</u> transgressions. ²Wash <u>me</u> thoroughly from <u>mine</u> iniquity, and cleanse <u>me</u> from <u>my</u> sin. ³For <u>I</u> acknowledge <u>my</u> transgressions: and <u>my</u> sin is ever before <u>me</u>. ⁴Against Thee, Thee only, have <u>I</u> sinned, and done this evil in Thy sight: that Thou mightest be justified when Thou speakest, and be clear when Thou judgest. ⁵Behold, <u>I</u> was shapen in iniquity; and in sin did <u>my</u> mother conceive <u>me</u>. ⁶Behold, Thou desirest truth in the inward parts: and in the hidden part Thou shalt make <u>me</u> to know wisdom. ⁷Purge <u>me</u> with hyssop, and <u>I</u> shall be clean: wash <u>me</u>, and <u>I</u> shall be whiter than snow. ⁸Make <u>me</u> to hear joy and gladness; that the bones which Thou hast broken may rejoice. ⁹Hide Thy face from <u>my</u> sins, and blot out all <u>mine</u> iniquities. ¹⁰Create in <u>me</u> a clean heart, O God; and renew a right spirit within <u>me</u>.

As we've arrived at the culmination of our 7-Part Detox Series, as I promised on last week, I want to conclude these sequences of sermons with the subject: *Lord, Clean This House from the Inside Out.*

On January 19th we started our journey toward 'authentic living' gleaning from the book *The 40 Day Soul Fast* authored by Cindy Trimm. By *authentic living*, we are talking about a life that is true to ourselves and more in line with what we were created to be versus one that is lived based upon who the world and others have told us to be. It is the difference between living a life of fiction or one that is non-fiction. *Fiction* means: invented, fabricated, manufactured— something that is make-believe, while *non-fiction* means: based on reality. I ask this question of everybody: "Are you being YOU, or is your life a script that somebody else wrote?"

We stated in the beginning, in the very first message of this series, *Operation Detox*, that; the object and focus of this 40-day fast was not so much the abstinence of food and beverage, but the elimination of toxic elements uncovered within us by us and discovered around us by us that were found to be detrimental or damaging to us, in terms of incapacitating our abilities to operate within life at maximum capacity or to embrace life in such a way that we enjoy life.

We stated in the beginning that many people cannot embrace life nor do they enjoy life simply because there is unrest on the inside caused by contamination lodged within the storage faculties of our mind, will, and emotions, which comprise our soul. In this, we stated that; what affects us on the inside will also impact the world around us, in terms of relationships, and in terms of attitude, character, conduct, communication, conversation, composure, and even appearance.

Somewhere during the course of these seven weeks we mentioned the fact that—if a person doesn't feel good about themselves, that same person would not invest much effort in themselves, in terms of how they look, dress, and in some cases, how they smell.

People plagued with low self-esteem are people, who tend to rely too much on the validation of others: what others say, what others think, and what others expect of and from them in order to feel good about themselves. But in our message, *We Are What We Think*, I told you; it matters not the evaluations or opinions of others about us, but more so than what they think, say, or expect of and from us is what we think and say about ourselves, in combination with, what we expect from and of ourselves. I stated that; it is our self-appraisal and not the contemplations or conversations of others that either make us or break us. We quoted British philosophical writer *James Allen*, who said, "We ourselves are makers of ourselves by virtue of the thoughts we choose and encourage."

Throughout this entire series I've sought to embed within each of us the realization that—we are in control of ourselves, and this control we cannot relinquish into the hands and authority of anyone else other than God. We've been saying you have to think for yourself, and feel for yourself, and speak for yourself, and validate yourself. Don't look to another to legitimize you—you legitimize YOU.

In sermon number three we ask the question, *Do You Want to Be Made Whole*, and we asked it because, as we stated in that message; it is difficult to help somebody who doesn't want to be helped. We said, *it is only when you decide for yourself that you need help and that you want help that you can be helped*. I can't help you if you don't want it, but if you what it, there is help. Our text is a cry for help. It is an appeal to God for intervention. It entreats God. It pleads with God. It implores God to 'clean this house from the inside out.'

Psalm 51 is a poetic soliloquy (So-LIL-oh-kwee) for soul surgery, inner cleansing, inward expungement, and for internal renovation. The petitioner places himself at the mercy of God and he is asking of God to forgive his sin and to change his life. This has been the goal of our 40 days of detox. It has been a mission of metamorphosis and a program of purification. It has been a quest to rid ourselves of all things toxic: toxic thoughts, and toxic words, and toxic relationships, and toxic desires, and toxic influences, and toxic behavior.

For 40 days we've been in treatment. For 40 days we've been in therapy. For 40 days we've been in counseling, and we've been analyzing ourselves from the inside out—from 'the inside out' because Jesus said: *"It is not what goes into us that defiles us, but what comes out of us that makes us unclean."* In Matthew 15:19 and Mark 7:21 He says, *"Evil thoughts, adulteries, fornications, murders, thefts, covetousness, wickedness, deceit, lewdness, an evil eye, blasphemy, pride [and] foolishness"* all proceed from the heart. In other words, everything we do and everything we say has its root on the inside. The inside is 'ground zero'. It is the base, or foundation, or the starting point for all else. Thus, if there are problems on the outside, it is the inside that needs work. It is the inside that is in need of detoxification or decontamination. The pollutants that taint our character, communication, and conduct are within, with the greatest of toxics being 'sin'. *Sin* is 'anything that is considered to be a transgression against Divine Law,' be it words, thoughts, or actions. *Sin* is poisonous to self. *Sin* is a virus to self. *Sin* is destructive to self. *Sin* is a disadvantage to our lives and relationship with God. Let's talk about *sin*.

I gleaned the subject of our sermon from a song by Isaac Carree entitled, "Clean this House," and like the psalm, this song is an appeal for forgiveness, cleansing, restoration and purging. Both the *psalm* and the *song* are confessionary prayers—both concede sin, and both seek the absolution or amnesty of God, as both talk about God taking away the impurities of sin that the *psalmist* and *songster* may be clean—from the inside out.

When you read the psalm and when you listen to the song, one can easily observe some parallels between the two, starting with the psalmist and the songster admitting guilt. It is the admission of guilt that is the first step toward recovery, rehabilitation, purification and remission. The theological term is 'confession'. *Confession* is the acknowledgement of wrongdoing. It is the recognition of misconduct and the declaration of delinquency. Before there can be *cleansing* there must be *confession*. In other words, self must drop a dime on self and self must concede the misconduct of self. Self must look at self and self must say to self, 'You need help', and until self dissects self and pleads guilty to all charges leveled against self, there can be no divine pardon or purification. But *"If we confess,"* the Bible says in 1st John 1:9, *"God is faithful and just to forgive us our sins, and to cleanse us from all unrighteousness."* We've got to come clean. In fact, if you want to be cleansed, you must come clean. In other words, if you are serious about God cleaning your house from the inside out, you must admit that it is dirty.

Psalm 51 is a Psalm of David, and it was written in the aftermath of being exposed by God through the prophet Nathan of an adulterous affair, which led to the murder of the husband of the woman he slept with. This is the story of 'David and Bathsheba', archived within Scripture in the Book of 2nd Samuel (Chapter 11). I'm uncertain as to the inspiration of the song by Isaac Carree, although allegations have been made of infidelity, but they are allegations without substantiation, thus, we will not analogize the sin of David to Isaac, although the lyrics to the song implicate some form of immorality: "I've been messing up," he says, "done lost my house, done lost my job, wife walking out?" "I've been smoking a lot, and drinking a lot, and all up in the club, I've been doing this, I've been doing that, and I had no business doing it." "No church or Bible study; ain't been in my Word. I know better than this, can't live my life in sin, we confess Him. Clean this house from the inside out." There is some form of immorality.

Immorality is *sin*, and sin is universal. The Bible says, *"All have sinned and come short of the glory of God." "There is none righteous, no, not one."* Thus, *Psalm 51* fits all of us, as all of us, like David, were *shaped in iniquity* and *conceived in sin*. Our sins may differ, but sin is widespread. In other words, my sins may not be your sins and your sins may not be mine, but each of us has something within us in need of elimination from us. In other words, each of us has some dirt spots in need of sweeping and each of us has some scandal in need of scrubbing. I said *scandal* because you like the show, but there's a little scandal in all of us.

I know we've completed the book, but the process must continue. The book got us started, but the program is not over. We've only just begun. Real treatment is unending. Real treatment is perpetual. Real treatment is abiding. Real treatment is unremitting. We cannot stop. We cannot relax. We cannot suspend or minimize our efforts. Like David, we must throw ourselves at the mercy of the Court. We must look to God and admit to God our sin against God. We must say, 'Lord, clean this house from the inside out.' Wash me. Cleanse me. Purge me and clear me. *"Blot out mine iniquity"* and *"hide Thy Face from my sins." "Create in me a clean heart"* and *"renew within me a right spirit."* Lord, Clean this house from the inside out.

I've lost my joy and I want it back. I've lost my song and I want it back. I've lost my shout and I want it back. I've been broken by sin—Lord, fix me up. Lord, clean this house from the inside out. Search me and sanctify me. Examine me and expunge me. Clean up my thoughts. Clean up my talk. Clean up my heart. Clean up my life. Lord, make me better. Lord, make me different. Lord, make me wiser. Lord, make me whole again.

I've come back to the Potter's House and I sit again on the Potter's Wheel. Take your Hands and mold me. Take your hands and reshape me. Take out the impurities. Take out the iniquities. Take out the indecencies. Take out all indiscretions. Lord, clean this house from the inside out. I surrender. Lord, clean this house from the inside out. I yield. Lord, clean this house from the inside out. I submit. I'm yours Lord. Everything I've got and everything I am, it's yours— from the top of my head to the sole of my feet, all unlike Thee, Lord take it out. Clean this house from the inside out.

I repent. I apologize. I did it and I admit it. I'm sorry. Forgive me. I'm sorry. Rekindle me. I'm sorry. Rinse me Lord. Clean this house from the inside out. Refurbish my thoughts. Detoxify my tongue. Purify my heart. Reorder my steps. Clean me up! I'm dirty. Clean me up! I'm unwashed. Clean me up! I'm polluted. Lord, clean this house from the inside out!

31 DAILY INSPIRATIONAL NUGGETS

DAY 1
PATIENCE

Patience is defined as "the ability to accept or tolerate delay, trouble, or suffering without getting angry or upset," and whether we realize it or not, there are real benefits in being patient. Patience refines and perfects us. It is a discipline we must practice if we want to break free from the myriad of things that can plague and pollute our soul. Impatience brings upon us all sorts of emotional and relational problems, such as losing our temper and saying things we will later regret. When we are impatient we become agitated, anxious, stressed, frustrated, angry, flustered, and so on. Without patience, we will not be able to cultivate other important characteristics, such as self-control, compassion, faithfulness, mercy, and love, among other attributes that comprise the *fruit of the Spirit* (Note: Galatians 5:22-23). Impatience causes us to get out of step with the Spirit of God, whose lead we are to closely follow. I say, get back in step, be patient with yourself, and especially with those around you. As God is patient with us, He also expects the same of us in our walk with others. The Bible says He is "longsuffering toward us" (2 Peter 3:9), which means that God suffers long with us. Scripture also declare, "Be not weary in well doing, for in due season, you will reap, if you do not give up" (Galatians 6:9). When we exercise patience, we exhibit a divine trait that is advantageous to us, both spiritually and naturally.

DAY 2
PEACE

PEACE, we all desire it, but do we practice it? Eleanor Roosevelt said, "It isn't enough to talk about peace, one must believe it, and it isn't enough to believe it, one must work for it." How does one work for it? The Bible says: "Do all that you can to live in peace with everyone" (Romans 12:18). In other words, cultivate what you expect. Be loving. Be compassionate. Be humble. Give up retaliation and sharp-tongued sarcasm. Instead, bless--that's your job, to bless. If you be a blessing you will get a blessing. You cannot expect peace being a hell raiser or a trouble maker. Jesus said, "Blessed are the peacemakers, for they shall be called the children of God" (Matthew 5:9). Hear what 1st Peter 3 teaches us: "Whoever wants to embrace life and see the day fill up with good, here's what you do: Say nothing evil or hurtful; snub evil and cultivate good; run after peace for all you're worth." What you desire, dispatch. SHALOM.

DAY 3
INSIGHT & EYESIGHT

Albert Schweitzer said, "The real art of discovery consists not in finding new lands but in seeing with new eyes." Many of us have not learned to see beyond how things look. We live in a material world that co-exists with a parallel spiritual dimension. All that we see and experience in the natural originates in the spirit. God wants to give us spiritual eyesight to see where and what others cannot, but we are only given this vision as we tune in to Heaven's frequency through prayer, fasting, and the study of God's Word. If you need a fresh perspective in life, trust God for insight and new eyesight. The Bible says, "Trust Him, and lean not to your own understanding [or perception], but in all thy ways acknowledge Him [God], and He shall direct your path" (Proverbs 3:5-6). It's time to see what others don't see and become your authentic self. You can never enjoy a 3D movie to its fullest without 3D glasses, and as such, you cannot fully grasp all that life has to offer without God. There is more to see than what you see and there is more to have than what you have. Scripture says, "Eyes has not seen, nor ear heard, nor have entered into the heart of man the things which God has prepared for those who love Him" (1 Corinthians 2:9, NKJV).

DAY 4
LIVING A DISCIPLINED LIFE

Today, the focus is on living a disciplined life. Too many people are living lives that are out of control, and yet, we seek the blessings of God upon our life and endeavors. We deceive ourselves. In order to receive from God, you must please God. An undisciplined life does not please Him. The Bible says, "No good thing will God withhold from the one whose life pleases Him" (Psalm 84:11). Practice discipline. As it profits the body when we exercise with such, so it is beneficial to the soul. Mohandas Gandhi said, "The main purpose of life is to live rightly, think rightly, and act rightly". Come on, you can do it. A disciplined life in God will produce the fruit of the Spirit: "love, joy, peace, patience, kindness, goodness, faithfulness, gentleness, and self-control." Ephesians 4:1-3 declares: "Get out there and walk—better yet, run on the road God called you to travel. Do this with humility and discipline and not in fits and starts, but steadily, pouring yourselves out for each other in acts of love." You are in control of you, now, take control and do the right thing!

DAY 5
UNIQUENESS

You are unique. God is a God of originality. As no two snowflakes are alike when they hit the ground, so you are a one-of-a-kind expression of God's glory. Never be ashamed of your gender, color, ethnicity, and the season of your generation. Take time to praise God for the magnificent tapestry that makes you who you are. You are fearfully and wonderfully made, a unique expression of God's image in the Earth realm. No one else has your DNA. Don't try to be anyone else. Be you. Do you. Celebrate you. In the history of the world no one else has ever been or ever will be just like you. Take some time out and inspect what makes you uniquely you and be grateful for the gift God created you to be. You are a gift. Rejoice in the wonder and majesty that is you. Look in the mirror and SMILE. You are special!

DAY 6
IMAGING & PASSION

The topic is IMAGING & PASSION. What is your imagery like? We were made in the image of God with the capacity to emulate divine characteristics, such as: Love, Compassion, Forgiveness, Mercy, Grace,

Goodness, Kindness, Patience, etc. These, and more, we should reflect in our daily living among others. Jesus said, "Let your light so shine before mankind that they may SEE your good works, and glorify God (your Father) in Heaven" (Matthew 5:16). I say, the world is in need of your divine light. Turn it on and illuminate your environment. In Sunday school we use to say/sing: "Brighten up the corner where you are." Show others what God really looks like. Give evidence that you are a child of God made in His image by showcasing divine attributes. You don't have to tell others what you are if you show others what you are. The term 'Christian' means "Christlike." Turn on your light. There is too much darkness in the world. Jesus said, "You are the light of the world" (Matthew 5:14). Flip the switch. Instead of 'lights out', I say, "Lights on!" It's been in the 'off' position too long. Turn on the light—now on to embracing your passion(s). It is passion that gives you eyes to see what is possible and the fortitude to pursue it. Your passions are those things that drive you to do and be more—those things that make you feel alive, cause you to forget limiting circumstances or perceived shortcomings, and enable you to feel the joy of doing something beyond yourself. Passion will cause you to take risks and stand against the odds. What is your passion(s)? Embrace it/them. Go after it/them—Dream big—Envision yourself doing something more and having more. Don't limit yourself and don't allow others to limit you. Get on your mark, get ready, get set—GO!

DAY 7
JOY

What brings you joy? *Joy* is defined as "a feeling of great pleasure and happiness." Joy is important within our lives, without which, our souls will not be healthy and we will not live life at our maximum potential, thus, we cannot allow anything or anyone to rob us of this valuable emotion. "Being joy-deprived is similar to, if not worse than, being sleep-deprived" (Cindy Trimm)! Sleep deprivation affects us in a negative way, slowing us down and sapping us of energy. Whenever we allow our joy to be stolen, we also lose our peace and there is a break down in our emotional immune system that leaves us vulnerable to attack. Maintain your joy. Guard it at all cost. Look to the Lord. Study His Word. Fortify your joy depository with prayer, and surround yourself with people who add to your joy rather than take it away. Again I ask, "What brings you joy?" Harness it. Treasure it, and spend more time with it. Remember, eliminate those things/people that would steal your joy, and if you need more of it, I recommend JESUS. In the words of Mr. Spock: "Live long and prosper."

DAY 8
BEAUTY

What is true beauty? It is what is left of us once we peel away the layers of artificial roles we so often play and the lies and limitations we so often impose on our own souls/selves. Too often we place too much emphasis on the surface, when in essence; the real value is within us. It is the beauty of your soul. "You, the real you, is a work of art" (Cindy Trimm). A divine masterpiece, crafted by the hands of God, created in His image and likeness, and fearfully and wonderfully made. Never doubt for a moment just how beautiful you really are. If only you could see what God sees? Never-mind the definitions this world gives for beauty. The Temptations were right in saying, "Beauty's only skin deep, yeah, yeah, yeah." It's alright to fix up the outside, but create some space in your life for a spiritual beauty spa. Soak in God's presence. Take a bath in His Word. Let Scripture wash you and the Spirit peel away the old, dead things of your life and soften the tough and rough places of your life. Psalm 96:9 says, "Worship the LORD in the beauty of holiness." Holiness looks good to God and holiness gains you the favor of God and entrance into His Eternal Home. The Bible says, "Holiness without which, no person shall see God" (Hebrews 12:14). The next time you grab for something artificial to put on your head, face, hands or feet, remember it's only

47

superficial. Invest more in the real you, the you that will put a smile on God's Face so you can hear Him say: 'You are so beautiful to Me.'

DAY 9
RECEPTION

How is your reception? God wants to communicate with us and He is communicating, and simply because you don't hear Him doesn't mean He's not speaking. Maybe you are tuned into the wrong frequency. Maybe something or someone is complicating or scrambling the signal. Think about the fact that everyday messages are passing through the atmosphere that are available to be picked up by radios, computers, telephones and televisions, but unless we have the appropriate receiver, we cannot intercept what's being transmitted. And as it is in the natural realm, so it is in the spirit realm. Sin corrupts our ability to properly hear what God is saying. When it is present we experience "call drops." But all is not lost. The remedy is confession. Confession reopens the communication and grants us the opportunity to hear without interference (Read 1 John 1:9). God is ready to download thoughts, answers, solutions, miracles, and ideas to you, but is things right in your life to receive? Are you ready to receive? Do you have a hearing problem? If so, there are some hearing aids available to enhance your ability to hear what God is saying called Apostles, Pastors, Teachers, Evangelists, and Prophets. God has given us His Word. The Bible says "Faith comes by hearing," and "How can they hear without a preacher?" You also have the channel of prayer. Use it. It is to your advantage. Don't miss what God is saying and doing in the Earth realm. Pick up your Bible, go to church, get in your prayer closet, and hear the language that will give you the needed inspiration, revelation, information, and instruction to make your life better. God is speaking, but are you listening?

DAY 10
AUTHENTIC LIVING

Are you being true to whom you are or are you denying who you are in favor of what others say you are? Are you pursuing and living your dream or someone else's? Are you living your life or the life crafted by others? Harvey S. Firestone said, "Accept no one's definition of your life, but define yourself." Nothing or nobody should define you—you should define you. Don't live life in falsehood or facade. Don't give others a vote on you. Maintain the integrity of you. You will never be happy masking your true self and the desires and goals you have for yourself. Shakespeare so aptly said, "To thine own self be true." In other words, don't imitate another but 'be yourself.' Be the best YOU that you can be. No one is better than you at being you. You are unique. No one else has your DNA. Cultivate your uniqueness and God-given originality. Do not compare yourself with anyone else. Do you. Set the standard for you. Step to the music you hear and let others step to what they hear. "Become your own choreographer and perfect your own moves, then seek out opportunities to show them off" (Cindy Trimm). Accept no limits. Lift every lid, and dare to go where no one has gone before. Reserve and exercise your divine right to be who God made you to be and to do what God has gifted you to do. The late John F. Kennedy said, "Let us resolve to be masters, not the victims, of our history, controlling our own destiny." Dare to live authentically. *Authenticity* simply means "being true to who you are." Are you doing YOU or someone else? I seek to be the greatest ME I can be! What about you?

DAY 11
FOCUS

"The number one thing that keeps people from realizing their goals, maximizing their potential, and fulfilling their purpose is focus" (Cindy Trimm). What do you envision for your life? It is that very thing you must focus on. Your focus determines your future. If you want to see something in your future, focus on that today. Focus is the key. Whatever you focus on today is given permission to exist tomorrow, be it good or bad. Today's inspirational advice is to: set your focus on where you want to go and not on where you came from. Concentrate on what you desire to accomplish and not on what you've failed to do. Zero in on your healing and not your sickness, on your deliverance and not your detriment, on what remains and not on what has been lost. Train your mind to focus on the positive if you wish to have positive results (Read Philippians 4:8). Wherever you place your attention, the rest of you will follow: talents, abilities, energies, and emotions. So, focus on your dreams, future, goals, and vision. Remember, your focus becomes reality.

DAY 12
REDEEMING TIME

The Bible says, "Redeem the time" (Ephesians 5:16). In this context the term 'redeem' means to make good use of time. In other words, we are to make every minute of every day count. Are you making every minute of every day count or are you wasting time with time-wasters? I could name some, but it would be better if you take an account of how you spend or allocate each hour of each day. Are you using time productively or are you wasting time? Peter Drucker said, "Until we can manage time, we can manage nothing else."

How ordered or orderly is your life? Are your days cluttered with junk activities? "Junk time is as bad as junk food" (Cindy Trimm). Both are unhealthy for us. Take some time to take stock of what consumes your time. Proverbs 4:26 says, "Consider well the path of your feet." What do you do? Where do you go? How much television claims your day? What about the Internet, video games, cell phone usage, texting, tweeting, Facebook, etc.? We all know that 'times flies', but Michael Altshuler states: "The good news is you're the pilot." Take control of your flight of time. Don't be prodigal with your time. It is a God-given gift and commodity. Use it wisely. Use it purposefully. What you do with it today is important for when tomorrow comes, this day will be gone forever, leaving in its place something that we have traded it for. What are you trading your time for? Are you gaining for it and are you better for it? Do we need more time—probably not. We simply need to make better use of the time we have. Don't utilize time carelessly. Plan your time and get the most out of it. We all have a day of birth and death with a 'dash' in between. My question to you is: What are you doing with your dash?

DAY 13
WHO AM I?

Have you ever asked yourself that question? Why am I here? What is my purpose in life? Apart from what you do and the roles you play, are you really being true to you or have you slipped into a life of mediocrity and dullness? Here's a quote worthy of pondering: "He who trims himself to suit everyone will soon whittle himself away" (Raymond Hull). The term "whittles" means, "to reduce, destroy, or wear away gradually." In many ways, this is the existence of so many who are sleepwalking through life because their only life is that which they live through others. If this is you I say, "Wake up!" It's time to live for you! It's time for you to embrace the life uniquely designed for you by God. You cannot live your total life walking in the shoes that others have picked out for you. Pick out your own! Embrace the importance of your own identity. Who are you? What are your passions? Do you have a dream or dreams? Will it or they become a reality? Are you striving to make your dreams possible or have you settled down into allowing the people around you to dictate to you who you are and what your life is all about? If this is you, again I say, "Wake up!" Don't settle. Don't whittle. Don't somnambulate. Live! "You are your Heavenly Father's child. You have His DNA imprinted in your spirit, encoded in your heart" (Cindy Trimm). Live!

Jesus said, "I am come that they might have life, and that more abundantly" (John 10:10). Grab hold of this truth. Believe it is so. Wrap your mind around what it means in regards to how you live. Set your thoughts on hearing from your heart. In a previous post I told you: "Step to the music you hear and let others step to what they hear." "To thine own self be true" (William Shakespeare). I cannot wait to see the outcome of the real you!

DAY 14
SELF-WORTH

If you were to paint a portrait of yourself, how do you see yourself? Do you see something worthy of framing and showcasing to the world, or would you hide what you paint for fear of what you see being rejected by others? Poor self-image and self-rejection has distorted the true beauty that is you. If you see what God sees, you will see that you are beautiful! The Bible says, "Man looks on the outward appearance, but God looks at the heart." Too many of us have allowed what others say about us or to us to deface and devalue our self-worth and self-esteem. However, it matters not the surveys that others conduct on us, but of greater value than their assessments are the appraisals we do on ourselves. In other words, what YOU think about YOU is more important than what others think or say about you. And even greater than self-evaluation or people-evaluation is God-evaluation. You were fearfully and wonderfully made by Him, and never doubt for a moment the wealth of the real you. You are so precious to God until He made provisions to redeem you unto Himself: "For God so loved the world that He gave His only begotten Son" (John 3:16). All of us deal with rejection. It is a part of life as there is no way we can possibly be what everyone wants us to be or what everyone likes. Don't worry about the rejections of others; just don't reject yourself, especially based on the rejections of others. Even Jesus was rejected. The Bible says, "He came unto His own and his own received Him not" (John 1:11). He is "the stone which the builders rejected" (Acts 4:11). Even though others may reject you, never doubt for a moment how much you mean to God. God loves you. You are His beloved. You have worth, value, merit, and significance. These words are somewhat synonymous, but I used them to emphasize the magnitude of your distinction. Start seeing yourself as God sees you and start saying to yourself: I am beautiful. I have worth. I am precious. I am beloved. Here is a Kathryn Stockett quote from the book and movie 'The Help': "You is kind. You is smart. You is important." Never be convinced otherwise.

DAY 15
EXPECTATIONS

Too often in life too many of us go through life striving to live up to everyone else's expectations of us, and in the process, who we really are and what we truly desire to be and accomplish gets lost in our quest to follow the blueprints of others drawn up by them for us. I wonder how many of us are doing what we actually want to be doing versus what we have always been told we should be doing. I wonder how many of us are living authentic lives in contrast to imitation lives? I wonder if you are being true to you and to the God who created you or are you a clone of someone else. A 'clone' is something that is made to look like something else, but no matter how closely it resembles that something else, it is still but a forgery of that something else. Don't go through life as a forgery. Be your authentic self. Stop allowing others to define you—define yourself. Design your own blueprint. Chart out your own path. Fulfill your own destiny. Find your own identity! Need help; ask God to show you—YOU. You cannot be true to yourself if you have not discovered yourself. The real you is not the role you play, or the title you wear, or the labels people use to describe you, but the real you is who God molded you to be! When you discover that, you discover the courage to be yourself. You have nothing to prove to anyone but God. His approval is all that matters. If He says *well done*, that's good enough. So shed the clothes that others have laid out for you, pick out your own, put them on, and "live out your God-created identity" (Cindy Trimm)! Final quote: "Your identity and your success go hand in hand. Many people sacrifice their identities by not doing what they really want to do. And that's why they're not successful" (Lila Swell).

DAY 16
GROWTH & PURPOSE

Are you in growth mode, if not, what is preventing you from growing? The focus today is on 'growth' and 'purpose'. The two go hand-in-hand. There can be no growth without purpose. It is purpose that drives us toward growth and accomplishment, without which, we have nothing to reach for, and without something to reach for, we live an existence of complacency and dullness. We were created on purpose and with purpose. Purpose is the reason why we are. In fact, everyone and everything in life has purpose. All living things have purpose, including you. Do you know what your purpose is? Dr. Myles Monroe says, "Where purpose is not known, abuse is inevitable." People who live lives without purpose have no clear goals and ambitions; they simply exist from day-to-day waiting to die. In fact, without purpose you are on death row, living a zombie existence, walking aimlessly through life, living life as it comes. On the other hand; people with purpose are driven to grow beyond where they currently are. They live lives that are deliberate, intentional, circumspect, and mindful. They have dreams and visions, and they chart their lives and invest their time and energies accordingly. People with purpose take risks. They are daring, adventurous, audacious and tenacious. "You will never grow unless you attempt things that you cannot do, take on challenges that seem impossible, and stretch your faith to accommodate your desire" (Cindy Trimm). David O. McKay says, "Find a purpose in life so big it will challenge every capacity to be at your best." I ask the question again, "Are you in growth mode?" Is your church in growth mode? Are your finances in growth mode? Are you living your life with purpose? If not, it's not too late to discover your purpose and step into your purpose. What is it that excites you? What is it that you are good at? It may be your purpose in life. If so, cultivate it. Invest in it. Perfect it, and by all means, pursue it. Life is too short and you don't want to live a life full of regrets. Do it! Seek it! Don't let anyone or anything hinder you. Get on your mark, get set—GO! Jump out of the aquarium of limited beliefs and start swimming in the ocean of unlimited possibilities. "You were never intended to live small, but to grow into the vastness of potential the entire universe offers" (Cindy Trimm). I pray this word helps you. Indeed, it has pushed me into the pursuit of even more than what I do and have. Let it push you too!!!!!!!

DAY 17
WORDS—WORDS—WORDS

Believe it or not, your words frame your world. In other words, they establish the direction of your life and orchestrate the events of your life. Proverbs 18:21 declare, "Death and life are in the power of the tongue." We were created in the image of God, and part of that image is the power that our words wield. As God brought into existence all that is by His utterance (Note Hebrews 11:3), so we are able to transform our environment through our selection of communication. Words have authority. They can either hurt or heal. They can either build up or tear down. They can either mend or worsen. They can either cheer or sadden. They can either bless or curse. It is vitally important that we be cautious in the use of our words, whether spoken to someone else or utilized in conjunction with our thoughts and feelings about ourselves. God has fixed the boundaries, what we sow we reap, even in the realm of our words, therefore, contemplate before you converse because; it comes back. What comes back—all that you send out via your words. Here's a thought: what you desire, speak it into existence. Speak it into the life of others and speak it into your own. Start today. Change your language and you change your life. Speak well of yourself and speak well of others. Let your words be a force for good and not evil. Let your words heal and not hurt, build up and not tear down, mend and not worsen, cheer and not sadden, and bless and not curse. Before you open your mouth, say this prayer to God: "Let the words of my mouth and the meditation of my heart be acceptable in Your sight, O LORD, my strength and my Redeemer" (Psalm 19:14). I speak life and blessings into your life, now 'say it forward' into the life of someone else. Think about what you are creating with your words! I was always taught, "If you don't have anything good to say, then don't say anything at all."

DAY 18
RESPONSIBILITY & OWNERSHIP

Too often in life we go through life blaming others for the unfulfilled dreams and failures of our lives, however; we alone are responsible for what does not happen in our lives, and in many situations, for what does. In other words, we alone are in control of the decisions and choices we make, no one else are responsible for these but us. The focus today is on 'responsibility' and 'ownership'. It's up to us to guard our own heart, to govern our own mindset, to harness our own thoughts, to discipline our own behavior, and to direct our own words. "No one else can take responsibility for your life, purpose, or destiny other than you" (Cindy Trimm). We cannot rest this responsibility on the shoulders of anyone else. God gives each of us the ability to respond as we so choose to whatever circumstance(s) arises in our lives. The degree to which we take responsibility and ownership for our own destinies will determine the degree to which we fulfill or fail to fulfill our purpose and arrive at our destinies, as well as to maximize our potential. You alone are responsible for not doing what you should and could do—no one else. It is only when we take ownership responsibility and leadership of our own choices, decisions, and desired destinies that we can move forward in the direction of our goals and obtain our desired destinies. Stop the blame game and take charge of your own life. Les Brown says, "Accept responsibilities for your life. Know that it is you who will get you where you want to go, no one else." My question to you is, 'Where is it you want to go?' The steering wheel is in your hands. Turn the car on, put the gear in drive, and take yourself to the places and positions in life you want to go. Don't give your wheel to anyone else. Take responsibility and ownership of your potential, strengths, weaknesses, gifts, talents, calling, mistakes, and even failures. Yes, your failures. Learn from your failures. Let your failures be stepping stones. All truly successful people have had them, we all have, but the true failure is in quitting when you fail. The idiom says, "If at first your don't succeed, try, and try again." Come on, you can do it! Your life is in your hands.

DAY 19
POTENTIAL

Locked within each of us is an unlimited resource of possibilities. The thing that prevents this reservoir of probabilities from surfacing is our own inabilities to believe in ourselves and the God who created us, and to see beyond our current occupations and situations into a future rich with hope and options. "Potential is unused and unrealized power to do and to become" (Cindy Trimm). It is latent qualities or abilities that may be developed, and once developed, qualities or abilities that can lead you/us into a place of greater success, fulfillment and accomplishment. Satirist Philip Adams says, "Most people can do extraordinary things if they have the confidence or take the risks. Yet most people don't." I agree with this in that; many of us never explore the hidden potential within us. We too often settle for the comfort of what we have and where we are without attempting something different and without aiming for something more. But "you can never become who you've been destined to become until you lose who you used to be" (Rex Crain), and may I add, until you expand yourself beyond yourself, and until you are willing to test the uncertain and untried by stepping out in faith and mustering up the courage to leave the shorelines of coziness and familiarity, and launch out into the deepness of the waters of what can be if you only apply yourself and invest your gifts and talents and treasures in what you believe is possible. The Bible says, "Now faith is the substance of things hoped for; the evidence of things not seen" (Hebrews 11:1). All of us, including YOU, have the potential to do all sorts of things, but the question becomes: 'Are you willing to awaken what is dormant within you?' I say, as Paul told Timothy, "Stir up the gift of God, which is in you" (2 Timothy 1:6). Impregnate yourself with something new, greater, different, and uniquely you. There is a baby or babies awaiting arrival. Do not abort them but give them life. Bring them out. Give birth to the future opportunities and livelihoods that are yours. The name is already selected; it is POTENTIAL. Can you envision what it looks like? I can.

DAY 20
SOWING & REAPING

The Bible says, "Be not deceived; God is not mocked: for whatsoever a man sows, that shall he also reap" (Galatians 6:7). In other words, we get in accordance with what we plant, either in produce, deed, or word. There is an inherent boomerang effect to everything that we send out. Proverbs 11:25 declare, "The liberal soul shall be made fat, and he who waters shall himself be watered." Every choice has a consequence and every seed has a harvest, be it good or bad. Jesus told Peter, "Put your sword in its place, for all who take the sword will perish by the sword" (Matthew 26:52). What is it you desire to flow into your life; you can have it, if you give it away. Love returns love, just as hate returns hate. Be a friend and you shall have friends. "Forgive, and you shall be forgiven" (Luke 6:37). "Give, and you shall get" (Luke 6:38). Be a blessing and you shall gain blessings. There is much in the wisdom of God's Word about the laws of sowing and reaping. Indeed, our seed determines our crop. If we expect much, we must sow much, but where we are scanty and stingy, we cannot look for abundance (Note: 2 Corinthians 9:6). Unknown to us, but well-known to God, is the bounty in every seed. Robert Schuller said, "Anyone can count the seeds in an apple, but only God can count the number of apples in a seed." Sowing and reaping is both a natural principle, as well as a spiritual one. If what you have is not what you need or desire, the problem is not your harvest, but your seed. The question becomes: What are you sowing? The question becomes: How much are you sowing? The question becomes: Where are you sowing? One lesson from Jesus' *Parable of the Sower* (Matthew 13; Mark 4; Luke 8) is that; the ground of your planting is as critical as the seed that you plant. The ground makes all the difference. Bad ground inhibits, but good ground enables. Find yourself some good ground and sow into it. Be known for that. Disseminate and you will acquire. Propagate and you will procure. It is written, "It is more blessed to give than to receive" (Acts 20:35), but know that; every giver will receive. This is a promise and divine law. What we sow, we reap. In proportion to what we sow, we reap. Here's a lesson from the financial world: No investments, no dividends. No deposits, no withdrawals. The seed is in your hand. Don't consume it, but plant it. Don't store it away, but plant it. If you eat the seed or hide the seed you should be planting, you nullify all future opportunities to have more than what you currently have. Sowing is Biblical, withholding is not. What do you need? Start sowing it today!

DAY 21
COMPASSION

Simply put, "Compassion is love in action. It comprises mercy, kindness, generosity, justice, and patience" (Cindy Trimm), and might I add, forgiveness. Compassion symbolizes the nature and heart of God. He is compassionate. He is merciful. He is kind. He is generous. He is just. He is forgiving, and indeed, God is patient. I thank Him for that. Compassion compels a person to involve him or herself in the sufferings of others, to do what he or she can to relieve or alleviate their pain, or trouble, or difficulty, or lack. It is more than the emotional feeling of sorrow for someone else, what compassion does is that it intercedes in the affairs of others, going beyond itself in sacrifice, concern, care and philanthropy, it does what it can to make life better for other people. Showing compassion, even to our enemies or others undeserving and ungrateful can make a difference, and it will only expand your stature in the sight of God. God is pleased when we open up our hearts and resources to those around us in benevolence and good will. In fact, He rewards us when we accommodate the needs of others (Note: Proverbs 19:17 & 28:27 & Matthew 25:31-46). What better way to share the love of God than to be a blessing of consolation and encouragement. Oftentimes we underestimate the power of a touch, a smile, a kind word, a meal, a warming coat, and boots, and gloves, and a hat, as well as a visit to the hospital, or prisons, or senior citizen facilities, or to the streets where so many call 'home'. Many times we fail to do the simplest of things that are the biggest of delight and satisfaction to others, and many times we neglect to go out of our way to brighten the day for someone else. I challenge you to be a Good Samaritan; to go out of your way to help someone along the way. Someone that is hurting. Someone that is helpless. Someone that is homeless. Someone that is hungry, for when you supply others their needs, God will supply you yours. You will never go hungry when you feed others. You will never be without assistance when you help others.

You will never be without shelter when you give such to others, and you will always be comforted when you comfort the afflictions of others. It is written in Ecclesiastes 11:1, "Cast your bread upon the waters, for you will find it after many days" (NKJV). One of my favorite songs is "If I Can Help Somebody." I leave you to ponder a portion of its lyrics: IF I CAN HELP SOMEBODY AS I PASS ALONG, IF I CAN CHEER SOMEBODY WITH A WORD OR SONG; IF I CAN SHOW SOMEBODY THEY'RE TRAVELING WRONG—THEN MY LIVING WILL NOT BE IN VAIN. Somebody needs your compassion today. Make your life count for something.

DAY 22
RESPECT

Respect is "A feeling of deep admiration for someone or something elicited by their abilities, qualities, or achievements". It means to "hold in esteem or honor." In fact, in the Bible the term 'respect' is used interchangeably with the word 'honor'. We are told to honor (respect) our parents, the elderly, those in authority, as well as one another (Note: Romans 12:10; 13:7 & 1 Peter 2:17). However, this seems to be a quality or attribute that is seriously lacking in today's society, where children disrespect their parents and or grandparents, students disrespect their teachers, parishioners disrespect their pastors, the young disrespect the old, and employees disrespect their employers. I know that in many situations what I just stated can also be stated in the reverse. In any case, disrespect demonstrates a disregard for what God, in His Word, commands us to do. It is also blatant disrespect for us to call people out of their names, to cuss people out, to belittle people, to embarrass people, and dismiss people as insignificant, as well as to be unaccepting of others simply because of race, creed, color, gender, age, nationality, or political affiliation. I must say; there is nothing acceptable or respectable about the use of the 'B' word, or the 'N' word, or the 'F' word, or any other obscene or profane language that disparages someone else. Whatever happened to the Golden Rule of treating people in the manner in which we would have people to treat us? We may not agree with what others say or do, and others may not think, look or behave like us, but we should respect the rights, opinions, and differences of others, as long as those differences don't infringe upon or undermine ours. The Bible teaches us to do all that we can to live peacefully with all people (Note: Romans 12:18 & Hebrews 12:14). Per the Urban Dictionary, *respect* means: valuing each other's point of view, being open to being wrong, accepting people as they are, not dumping on someone because you're having a bad day, being kind always, not dissing people because they're different to you and or from you, and not gossiping about people or spreading lies on people—RESPECT—it is showing consideration for someone else's feelings and interests, as well as being civil, courteous, reverent and polite. When we respect other people we exhibit a value for other people, the type of value that God places on all human life. Regardless of a person's locality or situation, the God way is R-E-S-P-E-C-T! We all want it. Let's give it.

DAY 23
LOYALTY

Loyalty is defined as "the quality of being loyal to someone or something." LOYAL—it is "giving or showing firm and constant support or allegiance to a person or institution." As I stated in Day 22; *respect* is lacking in today's society, but so seems to be 'loyalty'. There seems to be a shortage of people you can truly count on, depend on, relax with, and or put your trust in. Trust is given over to a person or people that are true to their word, and this must be proven before trust can be granted. A 'word' without affirmation or experience should not be so easily relied upon; first of all, "loyalty is evidenced by singleness of heart" (Cindy Trimm). The Bible says, "A double-minded man is unstable in all his ways" (James 1:8), meaning; a double-minded individual has divided loyalty, meaning; he or she is unsettled and he or she is untrustworthy. Thus, how can you trust a person who is not loyal? You can't. Disloyalty or unfaithfulness shatters trust, and once trust has been traumatized, it is difficult to restore. Not impossible, but difficult. Anyone in a relationship can attest to this. With most people, disloyalty or unfaithfulness is a turn-off. Per Proverbs 19:22 (NLT), what makes a person attractive is 'loyalty', not necessarily any of the superficial things we wear on the surface. On the surface you can dress well and smell good, and yet, still be unattractive if you are also wearing the garments of duplicity or deceit, or unreliability and unpredictability. I was always taught, *if a man doesn't have his word, he doesn't have anything,* so today I ask: How are you with your word? How trustworthy are you? How dependable are you? How reliable are you? Can God trust you? Can your Church, Temple, or Mosque trust you? Can your family trust you? Can your children trust you? Can your spouse trust you? Do you even trust yourself? It is difficult to trust people who are only devoted to themselves. "Loyalty is the pledge of truth to oneself AND others" (Ada Velez-Boardley). It is what keeps leaders in power, marriages intact, friendships unbroken, and trust unscathed. If you want to be counted as trustworthy, then be loyal to those in your circle of friendship, kinship, relationship, and membership. Loyalty is royalty. It is a treasure like none other. Don't betray the trust people may have in you—invest in it, protect it, embrace it, and cultivate it by being LOYAL.

DAY 24
LEGACY

It is what we leave here after we leave here. It is what we pass on to those who come after us. It is what we 'will' to our children, and our children's children, and that part of us, which lives on after we are dead. Know that, we are not just here for the present generation, but we are also here to impart an imprint (distinguishing influence and effect) for future generations. God desires from our lives something that will continue on after we are no longer on this Earth—something that will assist and inspire future generations and something that will ultimately bring glory to God. Know that, in all we do and say we emboss our fingerprint, and imbedded in our fingerprint is something about us that differentiates us from everybody else. With each person we touch we pass along something of us, be it good or bad, and each person we touch will in turn touch someone else, thus, passing along to them an action or word received from us. This, in essence, becomes a part of our legacy, that which continues on after we are gone. The question becomes: 'What are we passing on?' I would hope it is something positive, constructive, helpful and impactful. I would hope we consider what we do now, in terms of, what affect it will have on others later, especially on our sons and daughters and on their sons and daughters, and on our communities, churches, temples, and mosques.

I would hope our living will not be in vain. I would hope that we would not pass on any example of dysfunction, corruption, wickedness, or foolishness. I would hope we would not be too soon forgotten because we did nothing but exist. We all must leave here and we write our own eulogies; it is our own lives that preach the real message of our funerals. Don't go to the grave leaving the living searching without success to find something good to say about you. Your life speaks, but what will it say? We all don't have the same amount of years on Planet Earth, and it's not the number of years that truly matters, but what we do with the years we are granted by our Creator. It's not the longevity of life, but the quality of life. I leave you with this thought to ponder: After you are dead and gone, what will be your LEGACY? What will people say about you when you are no longer here? Will they even talk about you, or even miss you? The pen is in your hand—what is your story? How will it read? What will it say?

DAY 25
TEMPERANCE

It is one of the nine fruit of the Spirit (Galatians 5) that should be cultivated in the life of a Christian. It means 'self-control' or 'self-restraint'. It is the exercise of moderation, which is the avoidance of excess or extremes in one's life. Temperance requires self-discipline, which is the ability to control one's feelings and overcome one's weaknesses, and the ability to pursue what one thinks is right despite temptations to abandon it. So many areas of our lives would be far better if we get control of ourselves—of what we say, do, eat, drink, etc. The Bible advocates temperance and urges us to do all things in moderation. Proverbs 16:32 says, "Moderation is better than muscle, self-control better than political power." Think about what sins could have been avoided (and still can) and what pitfalls averted if we had only utilized self-control. "Great leaders have fallen because of their lack of self-control" (Cindy Trimm), and "accomplished men and women of God have compromised their faith and ministry simply because they were unable to exercise restrain" (Cindy Trimm). When I think about it, I don't know if it's a matter of unable or unwilling. We are in control of ourselves. No one controls us but us. Everything we do or fail to do is a matter of choice. We just need to make wiser decisions and better choices, which is why we need to seek the wisdom of God in all we do and say before we act and speak. James 1:5 declares, "If any lacks wisdom, let him ask of God, who gives to all liberally and without reproach." Proverbs 3:5-6 says, "Trust, and lean not to thine own understanding; in all thy ways acknowledge God, and He shall direct your path." Who better knows what is behind the door of our choices but God? Look to Him. Learn how to say 'no' to some things no matter what it looks like, feels like, smells like, or talks like. Remember, it was the lack of self-control that got us expelled from the Garden of Eden and introduced our flesh to the grave. All of us are tempted, however; temptation is not the sin, but giving in to our temptations is. Temperance will help us to live a victorious life.

DAY 26
MORALITY

It is "behavior or qualities judged to be good that are based on a set of principles concerning the distinction between right and wrong or good and bad conduct." Who determines what is right and wrong or good and bad? I say it is God, and His standards for such are set forth in His Word, we call it "The Holy Bible." We cannot exist in a society where there are no rules of morality. This leads to anarchy, which is a state of disorder caused by the absence of authority or laws. Where there are no laws there is only chaos (read the Book of Judges), which is total confusion and mayhem. The Bible says, "God is not the author of confusion, but of peace" (1 Corinthians 14:33), and where God is recognized as the Supreme Authority and His laws referenced and reverenced as such, peace will abide, for sin is defined. We don't like to talk about sin, however; sin is anything done contrary to the will of God—ANYTHING! It is "an immoral act that is considered to be a transgression against divine law." I know we live in a society where people make up their own laws of morality, but until we get back to utilizing God's law as the guideline for living, we will continue to spiral downward in the path of the cities of Sodom and Gomorrah. If you didn't know, these ancient cities were destroyed for their lack of morality. America was founded on the principles of divine law, but has since failed in its obligations to abide by divine law, and we see what is happening in America and to America. We need to get back to becoming a theocratic government. A *theocratic government* is a God-ruled government. We like to throw His name around, but when you examine His commandments and compare them to our conducts, there is very little resemblance, and God is not pleased. In a theocratic government (God-ruled), people treat each other better. In a theocratic government (God-ruled) the poor are provided for. In a theocratic government (God-ruled) the hungry are fed. In a theocratic government, the judgments are fair and equal for all of its citizens, not one for one group of people and another for all the rest. If we can just get back to living life on God's terms our homes, schools, neighborhoods, and churches would be so much better. All I want to say is; it pays to live right, and right is determined by God and not the White House, the court house, or any other house other than the House of God. No amount of legislation can eradicate or replace what God requires of us. What does The Lord require of us? Good question, but it is asked and answered in Scripture; it is "to do justly, to love mercy, and to walk humbly with our God" (Micah 6:8). The two greatest commandments are these: "Love the LORD with all your heart, mind, soul, and strength" and "Love your neighbor as yourself." The Apostle Paul put it best in his summarization of the love law: "Love does no harm to a neighbor" (Romans 13:10). If we can live by this, the world would be a much different world.

DAY 27
CAN WE DANCE?

Life has several elements in common with pair figure skating and ballroom dancing. There is *energy* in *synergy* that does not exist within the realm of individual effort. Not that individual effort is unworthy of merit and magnificence, but there is an even greater beauty watching two people in sync with each other, relying on each other, trusting in one another, who are dancing together in harmony, symmetry, and unity toward a collective goal. On the ice, "the woman is lifted, whirled, and thrown by the gifted and able-bodied partner that she trusts completely" (Cindy Trimm), and they are judged, not as two, but as one, and it is as one that they compete to win. Neither stands out above the other. On the dance floor, "all eyes are usually on the woman who is framed and supported by her partner" (Cindy Trimm), however; "without her partner, there would be no performance. It takes both the lead and the one being led to complete the dance" (Cindy Trimm), and here again, they are judged, not as two, but as one. Wouldn't it be nice if we could complete each other rather than compete against one other? Wouldn't it be nice if in our homes, churches, neighborhoods, legislation halls, cities, states, and nations we could dance, not in rivalry, but in synergy? Wouldn't it be nice for the races? Wouldn't it be nice for the sexes? Wouldn't it be nice for the country? Wouldn't it be nice for the world? Can we dance? In other words, can we work together? Can we worship together? Can we talk together? Can we live as one? Rodney King said it best, "Can we all just get along?" "No man is an island" (John Donne). We were created for community, and it is in community effort that we have the greatest and more efficient accomplishments. The Bible says, "Two are better than one, because they have a good return for their labor. If either of them falls down, one can help the other up. But pity anyone who falls and has no one to help them up" (Ecclesiastes 4:9-10). Can we dance? Life is too short to dance alone and it feels a lot better to have someone to dance with. But unless our dancing is linked together and in sync together, we dance together in vain. This applies to our homes. This applies to our churches, temples or mosques. This applies to our neighborhoods, and in every other arena of life. I hear the music and I love to dance, but not alone. I am looking for a dance partner; do you care to dance?

DAY 28
TOLERANCE

"Tolerance is the ability to accept the differences of others" (Cindy Trimm). It is that which enables us to be patient with others, compassionate of others, and charitable to others, regardless of the fact that we are different from others. This does not mean that we accept and excuse immoral behavior or unethical dealings, but simply that; we respect each other's God-given right to choose the path or paths we take in life. In some ways, being tolerant can be an effective tool in evangelism. The Apostle Paul says, "I become all things to all people that I may by some means win some" (1 Corinthians 9:22). It was Jesus' tolerance of marginalized people that attracted many of them to Him: prostitutes, winebibbers, tax-collectors, the sick, afflicted and diseased, the poor, criminals, old people, young people, widows and orphans. Many of these were treated by society and the religious elite as outcasts unworthy of association, but not so with Jesus. These were the ones He reached out to with the grace, love, and kindness of God, and we too should do the same, lest we forget that such were many of us. Many of us bore the traits of marginalization, but God was tolerant of us, not willing that any of us should perish. He loved us in our mess and He wooed us by being tolerant of us. It is tolerance, not judgment, that draws, and it is through tolerance that we display and disperse the true heart of God. Jesus said, "It is not the healthy who need a doctor, but the sick" (Luke 5:31). Never underestimate the power of tolerance. It can change hearts, circumstances, environments, and conducts. If it did it with us, it can do it with others. Think about it, and then exercise it. Though people are different from us, be tolerant. Remember, you are different to them too, and God loves all of us just the same.

DAY 29
ETHICS

This deals with the moral principles that govern our behavior; it is our value system or rules of conduct. It is what we live by, act on, respond to, and rely upon as the basis for our choices and decisions within life. Many people go through life without any moral compass to guide them. Many of our children have none in the home and are going through life without any clear distinction between what is right and what is wrong. Without a moral compass immorality runs rampant and the line of variance between good and evil is blurred. This is what is happening within our nation of America, as laws are being passed to legalize what is divinely immoral. This is vastly becoming the day and land where and when people make up their own standards of morality and where we allow government and governmental officials to outline for us what is ethical or not, however; as Christians, the Bible is our moral compass. The Bible is our manual for living and the guidebook we must familiarize ourselves with and govern ourselves by. It is "God-breathed and is useful for teaching, rebuking, correcting and training in righteousness" (2 Timothy 3:16). Always has and always will be. It is not the White House, the Governor's Mansion, City Hall, or the Legislative Chambers that define or determine morality, but it is God. We must look to Him in His Word and no one else, and then we must abide by His rules as outlined in His Book. If we do so, this world would be a far better place to live. We would treat each other better, respect each other better, assist each other better, as we would be better people ourselves, who value our own lives, as well as the lives of others, loving God and loving one another. God gave us Ten Commandments, 4 that address our relationship to Him and 6 that address our relationship to each other. Let us not continue to remove them from our public buildings and private dwellings. Let them remain in our nation, schools, homes, churches, and hearts as the barometer of behavior and the commandments of conduct. *So they are written, so let them be done.*

DAY 30
INTERDEPENDECE

This has to deal with mutual reliance and interconnection. As we are birthed into the world, we are birthed into a realm of dependency as we rely on others to nurture and nourish us until we become independent of such need. Independency is the stage of adolescence when we begin to make the difficult transition from the dependency of childhood to the independency of adulthood. Some take longer than others, but once we are here (adulthood), we cannot forget that we had help to get here, and now is the time to give back. Now is the time to be to others what others were to us. I would be foolish to think that I am what I am, have what I have, and are able to do what I am able to do without the intervention, sacrifice, support, and mentoring of people who took the time to impart into me of their resources, time, talents, experience, knowledge, love, patience, and wisdom. I have sense enough to know that I am standing on the shoulders of parents, grandparents, pastors, churches, teachers, friends, older siblings, civil rights leaders and workers, and even strangers who paved the way with blood, sweat, tears, money, and so much more, and for them and this I am truly grateful, and you should be too. None of us are disconnected from the rest of us. All of us are connected in some way, and knowing this, we should do our part, as others have done, to leave our imprint on the heart and in the lives of others, making their lives better, brighter, lighter, and more fulfilling, as others have done for us. Don't fool yourself, "we need each other to complete one another" (Cindy Trimm). Each of us are a puzzle piece of humanity, and as with any puzzle, each piece is important. Dr. Martin Luther King, Jr. said, "I can never be what I ought to be until you are what you ought to be. This is the way our world is made. No individual or nation can stand out boasting of being independent. We are interdependent." In other words, we are mutually reliant upon each other. "Together we stand, but divided we fall." As we come to the end of another Black History Month and one day away from the final day of our 40-day soul fast, let us not forget the contributions of those before us. Let us pay tribute to them, and the best tribute we can pay to them is to 'pay it forward'. In other words, as we have been the beneficiaries of the generosities and oblations of others, let's take from them, but pass what we've received onward to someone else. Let us not be hoarders. Let us share what has been shared and let us impart into others what has been imparted into us: faith, love, grace, mercy, forgiveness, kindness, benevolence, knowledge, truth, experience, wisdom, patience, and all other things invested in us. It was an investment. Patti LaBelle says, "When you've been blessed, pass it on." Always remember: we are standing on somebody else's shoulders and somebody else needs a shoulder to stand on. Give them yours. Help them to be what others helped us to become.

DAY 31
COMMUNITY

What do you think of when you think of community? The most common definition is: "a group of people who live in the same area, such as a city, town, village, or neighborhood," or "a group of people who have the same interests, religion, race, etc." Whatever your definition, community is important. Community offers camaraderie, friendship, fellowship, companionship, safety, security, and serves as a good support network. In community there is a sense of belonging that can lead to happier and healthier living. Isolation and separation breeds loneliness and depression, not to mention the increased possibilities of violence, substance abuse, mental illness, and other detrimental things that tend to exist when there is a breakdown of community or when people are detached from other people. In this age of technological advancement, busy schedules, and constant relocation of homes, jobs, churches, etc., it is becoming increasingly harder to feel any sense of community. People don't get together as they/we use to, even in the home there is an absence of community around the dinner table. Everybody eats at different intervals and in different quarters of the house. We each watch separate programs on TV in separate rooms, and we rarely communicate with each other. Even in our churches community is diminishing. Churches have simply become places where we worship together but do not fellowship together. In fact, after the benediction it is off to the races. We are so outta there we barely say 'goodbye'. Do we even know one another? I remember community when I was growing up. Everybody knew everybody and everybody spoke to everybody. We shared with each other, cared for one another, stood by each other, and looked out for one another's properties, as well as one another's families. If one of us had we all had. We had a bond then that exists now, even though we may no longer live on the same block. I could name many of those families even now. We were community and proud of it. We played ball together, went to school together, played hide-and-seek together, and just enjoyed each other's company. Where has those days gone? If ever there was a time for community revitalization, that time is now. It took a village to raise a child then and it still requires a village to raise a child now. We need community. It is needed in our neighborhoods. It is needed in our churches, temples and mosques. It is needed in our homes. It is needed for our children, widows, and senior citizens. Strong communities make for a strong and safer society. If our communities are to be better, we must become community again. In other words, we must not only live together, but we must also work together and be concerned for one another. This concern starts with communication. We must speak to each other. "Hello", my name is 'Larry', what's yours? I leave you with this quote: "When strangers start acting like neighbors... communities are reinvigorated" (Ralph Nader).

Look for these other Books, Workbooks & Manuals
By
Rev. Dr. Larry A. Brookins

Becoming a Five-Star Church:
Transforming the Church into a Ministry of Excellence

Becoming a Five-Star Member:
Answering the Call of "All Hands on Deck"

Discipleship: From Bond Leather to Shoe Leather

The Tabernacle: Where Humanity Meets Divinity

Evangelism: The Church in Sync with God

The Fruit of the Spirit: A Cluster of Christ-like Characters

Gifts of the Spirit: Divine Endowments for the Body of Christ

The Biblical Deacon Training Manual

The Deaconess Training Manual

Seven Things that God Hates & Seven Letters to Seven Churches

It's all about the Kingdom, Volume One

Seven Things that God Hates Companion Workbook

Seven Letters to Seven Churches Companion Workbook

Understanding the Ordinances of Baptism & the Lord's Supper

Lord, Teach Us to Pray: Gleaning from the Instructions of Jesus

Tithing: A Workbook on Biblical Giving

Teamwork Makes the Dream Work: Benefits
of Partnership & Collaboration

ALSO AVAILABLE: Sermon CDs, DVDs and Manuscripts

www.labrookinsministries.org

WHEN IN CHICAGO WORSHIP
OR STUDY WITH US

True Foundation Transformation Church
8801 South Normal Avenue •
Chicago, IL 60620 • (773) 994-8896
www.tftchurch.org
Sunday Service: 11 AM • Sunday School: 9:45 AM
Adult and Youth Bible Studies: Thursdays at 7 PM

TELECAST
Chicago Cable TV 36
Wednesdays: 9:30 – 10:30 PM •
Thursdays: 11:30 AM – 12:30 PM

LIVE & ON DEMAND WEBCAST
www.holyconnection.tv or www.tftchurch.org
Live Streaming:
Sundays at 12:00 PM (CST)
Thursdays at 7:15 PM (CST)

<u>PRAYER LINE</u>
1-605-475-4000, Access Code: 194158#
Monday thru Friday, 6 – 7 AM & 12 - 1 PM (CST)

Please feel free to share your comments with Rev. Dr. Larry A. Brookins or for inquiry about other material: <u>pastorbrookins@sbcglobal.net</u>

Visit us on the Web:

www.labrookinsministries.org